GEOGRAPHY

Curriculum Bank

KEY STAGE ONE
SCOTTISH LEVELS A-B

GEOGRAPHY

CANTERBURY COLLEGE

D1407234

SIMON ASQUITH

Published by Scholastic Ltd,
Villiers House,
Clarendon Avenue,
Leamington Spa,
Warwickshire CV32 5PR
Text © 1997 Simon Asquith
© 1997 Scholastic Ltd
2 3 4 5 6 7 8 9 0 7 8 9 0 1 2 3 4 5 6

AUTHOR
SIMON ASQUITH

EDITOR
IRENE GOODACRE

SERIES DESIGNER
LYNNE JOESBURY

DESIGNER
LOUISE BELCHER

ILLUSTRATIONS
MICK REID

COVER ILLUSTRATION
GAY STURROCK

INFORMATION TECHNOLOGY CONSULTANT
MARTIN BLOWS

SCOTTISH 5–14 LINKS
MARGARET SCOTT AND SUSAN GOW

Designed using Aldus Pagemaker
Printed in Great Britain by Ebenezer Baylis Ltd,
Worcester

British Library Cataloguing-in-Publication Data
A catalogue record for this book is available from the
British Library.

ISBN 0-590-53400-9

Contents

ACKNOWLEDGEMENTS

The publishers gratefully acknowledge permission to reproduce the following copyright material:

HMSO for reproduction of map outlines and text from the National Curriculum for Geography (1995) © Crown Copyright.

The author wishes to thank his wife, Karen,
and his daughter, Charlotte, for their incredible
patience and understanding.

Introduction

Scholastic Curriculum Bank is a series for all primary teachers, providing both an essential planning tool for devising comprehensive schemes of work as well as an easily accessible and varied bank of practical, classroom-tested activities with photocopiable resources.

Designed to help planning for and implementation of progression, differentiation and assessment, *Scholastic Curriculum Bank* offers a structured range of stimulating activities with clearly-stated learning objectives that reflect the programmes of study, and detailed lesson plans that allow busy teachers to put the ideas into practice with the minimum amount of preparation time. The photocopiable sheets that accompany many of the activities provide ways of integrating purposeful application of knowledge and skills, differentiation, assessment and record-keeping.

Opportunities for formative assessment are highlighted where appropriate within the activities, while separate summative assessment activities give guidelines for analysis and subsequent action. Ways of using information technology for different purposes and within different contexts, as a tool for communicating and handling information and as a method for investigating, are integrated into the activities where appropriate and more explicit guidance is provided at the end of the book.

The series covers all the primary curriculum subjects with separate books for Key Stages 1 and 2/Scottish Levels A–B and C–E. It can be used as a flexible resource with any scheme to fulfil National Curriculum and Scottish 5–14 requirements and to provide children with a variety of different learning experiences that will lead to effective acquisition of skills and knowledge.

SCHOLASTIC CURRICULUM BANK GEOGRAPHY

The *Scholastic Curriculum Bank Geography* books aim at providing teachers with a comprehensive coverage of the primary geography curriculum. These activities are designed to stimulate the learning and practice of geographical skills according to a range of themes and in the context of a range of places. The books aim to help teachers focus on planning teaching in and about their own school's local area, as well as the contrasting localities which have to be taught in these key stages.

There is one book for Key Stage 1/Scottish Levels A–B which provides coverage of early geographical skills using the school grounds and local area, study of a contrasting locality and the thematic study on environmental quality. There are two books for Key Stage 2/Scottish Levels C–E. *Places* focuses on place study and concentrates on using the local area and learning about contrasting UK and overseas localities, *Themes* concentrates on the topics of Rivers, Weather, Settlement and Environmental Change.

Bank of activities

This book provides a bank of activities which may be used in many different ways – to form a framework for a scheme of work; to add breadth and variety to an existing scheme; or to supplement a particular topic. Each activity can be used as a 'stand alone' exercise, but there is also progression between many of them.

Fieldwork

Fieldwork is an essential component of children's learning about places. Knowledge of any place is always more meaningful if it is based on direct experience and it is important that children are provided with experiences which give them opportunities for direct observation, collection and recording of primary data.

The children should be taken, on a regular basis, out of the classroom, into their own locality, and occasionally into other localities. Several activities require the teacher to arrange excursions into the local area and others rely on children working in and around the school grounds. It is important that children are well acquainted with the places they are allowed to go within school and that you check the school policy for taking children out of school. Extra adult help may sometimes be necessary.

Activities which require children to work outside the classroom, but within the school grounds, are marked with the ⬦ icon. Activities where children will be working outside the school grounds will have the ⬦ icon.

What is a locality?

Your own locality is considered to be your school and the immediate environs within easy access. It is best to restrict the area so that the children can feel 'ownership' of it.

For the purpose of several of the activities the locality of your school should include a variety of human and physical features. Contrasting localities should be of a similar size to your own locality.

Lesson plans

Detailed lesson plans, under clear headings, are given for each activity and provide material for immediate implementation in the classroom. The structure for each activity is as follows:

Activity title box

The information contained in the box at the beginning of each activity outlines the following key aspects:

▲ *Activity titles and learning objective:* For each activity, a clearly-stated learning objective is given in bold italics. These learning objectives break down aspects of the programme of study into manageable, hierarchical teaching and learning chunks, and their purpose is to aid planning or progression. These objectives can be easily referenced to the National Curriculum and Scottish 5–14 requirements by using the overview grids at the end of this chapter (pages 9 to 12).

▲ *Class organisation/Likely duration:* Icons †† and ⏱ signpost the suggested group sizes for each activity and the approximate amount of time required to complete it.

▲ *Fieldwork:* Where the activity requires or suggests that the teacher takes the children beyond the school gates, the activity will be flagged with a ⬘ icon. Activities within the school grounds have the ⬗ icon.

Previous skills/knowledge needed

Information is given here when it is necessary for the children to have acquired specific knowledge or skills prior to carrying out the activity.

Key background information

This section provides some background information on the geography covered by the activity. It should help the teacher understand the context of what is being taught.

Preparation

Advice is given for those occasions where it is necessary for the teacher to prime the pupils for the activity, prepare materials or set up a display or activity ahead of time.

Resources needed

All of the materials needed to carry out the activity are listed, so that either the pupils or the teacher can gather them together easily before the lesson begins.

Certain resources which are important for good primary geography teaching are referred to repeatedly. These include:
▲ a large-scale map of the school's locality;
▲ a British Isles map;
▲ a world map and globe.

What to do

Easy-to-follow, step-by-step instructions are given for carrying out the activity, including (where appropriate) suggested questions for the teacher to ask the pupils to help instigate discussion and stimulate investigation.

Suggestion(s) for extension/support

Ideas are given for ways of providing easy differentiation where activities lend themselves to this purpose. In all cases, suggestions are provided as to how each activity can be modified for less able children or extended for more able children. Activities which can be used or adapted for children with a variety of special educational needs are also indicated here.

Assessment opportunities

Where appropriate, opportunities for ongoing assessment, during or after a specific activity, are highlighted. Some photocopiable sheets can also be used in a summative way – these are indicated by the ⬖ icon.

Opportunities for IT

Suggestions are made as to how IT might enhance the activity or be directly utilised within it. Regular use of the computer is encouraged for the collection, handling and presentation of data gathered as a part of geographical work. The chart on page 159 presents specific areas of IT covered in the activities, together with more detailed support on how to apply particular types of program. Selected lesson plans offer more comprehensive guidance on the application of IT, these are indicated by bold page numbers on the grid, and the ⬘ icon at the start of the activity.

Display ideas

Where they are relevant and innovative, display ideas are incorporated into activity plans and illustrated with examples.

Other aspects of the Geography PoS covered

Any other parts of the Key Stage 1 Programme of Study covered by the activity are given here, using the referencing used in the National Curriculum document.

Reference to photocopiable sheets

Where activities include photocopiable activity sheets, small reproductions of these are included in the lesson plans, together with guidance notes for their use and, where appropriate, suggested answers.

Assessment

The 'Assessment' chapter includes a number of short activities with photocopiable sheets which can be used to assess summatively. The activities in this chapter have all been designed to allow children to do them individually and with little introduction.

In addition reference is made to other activity worksheets which can be used for summative assessment.

Photocopiable activity sheets

Most of the activities are accompanied by at least one photocopiable activity sheet. Some of these sheets are in direct support of the activity or form part of the activity, others provide necessary information and techniques or introductory or follow-up opportunities. Many of the sheets have been designed to be generic, so that teachers in any school will be able to use them within the context of their own school's local area and the contrasting localities that they decide to study with their pupils.

Cross-curricular links

Cross-curricular links are identified on a simple grid cross-referencing the particular areas of study in geography to the programmes of study for other subjects in the curriculum (see page 160).

GEOGRAPHY AT KEY STAGE 1

Geography is an essential part of every child's education. If taught well it should encourage and develop the natural sense of wonder that young children have about the world in which they live. It should help them answer their own questions about their surroundings and should stimulate a desire for ever-increasing knowledge and understanding of the world and the people in it.

During the Key Stage 1 and 2 years, geography should encourage children to ask questions about their world. They should be helped to learn where places are and what it might actually be like to live there. At Key Stage 1 the emphasis will be on the people who live in a place and what their lives are like. Children will begin to understand geographical concepts as they learn about other localities and their inhabitants. Key geographical concepts for young children are:

▲ location (where is the place being studied?);

▲ patterns (why are things where they are in this place?);

▲ processes (why is the place as it is?/how is it changing?/how is it connected to other places?).

Children should be directed towards looking for similarities and differences in different localities. The easiest approach is to let them compare their own local area with other places of a similar size. They should, by now, be forming the ability to 'know a place well' and recognise that there is such a thing as a 'sense of place'. They should also start to recognise that people who live in other areas may have different cultures, different sets of values and different attitudes towards the issues they face.

This book encourages children to develop the skills that will support them in their study of geographical themes in different places.

The activities in this book are designed to encourage children to ask questions about places, people and the inter-relation between them. Discussion is of vital importance and time should always be allowed for talking in groups.

As this book is written with a national readership in mind it is impossible to relate exercises to specific places. However, activities should be carried out in the context of real issues in your own locality wherever possible – it is always worth including ongoing issues in your neighbourhood or region and involving the children in real enquiry.

Many of the activities are practical in nature and should encourage the children to make decisions about real places and problems. First-hand experience is vital with young children, as is the experience of working socially with other children in groups of varying sizes.

Many activities require some recording by the children either through drawing, writing or other means. The teacher should decide the amount of written recording that the children should produce.

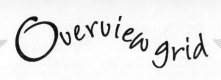

Learning objective	PoS/AO	Content	Type of activity	Page
Early geographical skills				
To encourage children to explore their own surroundings.	3a. *Aspects of the physical and built environment: Level B.*	Sketching and identifying sketches in the school grounds.	Fieldwork in school grounds. Paired sketch work.	14
To help children become familiar with geographical vocabulary.	3a. *As above.*	Matching simple words to pictures of places.	Classroom activity. Cutting and sticking.	15
To encourage an awareness that places are of different sizes and are referred to by different geographical terms.	3a. *As above.*	Modelling settlements of different sizes to assist learning of place types.	Group work. Box modelling.	17
We can follow directions to find a route or place.	3c. *Making and using maps: Level A.*	Making and following simple routes using geographical terms.	Playground, hall or field route game.	19
To develop fieldwork skills within the school's locality.	3b. *As above: Level B.*	Using sketching skills to create routes around locality.	Fieldwork. Sketching activity. Walk around school area.	20
To observe and record school surroundings. To use fieldwork skills to create a database about the school buildings and grounds.	3b. *Physical and built environment: Level B.*	Recording simple external details of the school building.	Fieldwork. Recording by drawing.	22
To provide children with simple fieldwork data collection skills.	3b. *Recording and presenting: Level B.*	Counting the numbers of people moving about in different parts of the school.	Fieldwork in school grounds. Timing and counting activity. Simple data collection.	24
To use sources other than first-hand experience to obtain geographical information.	3f. *Collecting evidence: Level B.*	Looking for information in estate agents' details.	Rôle play, reading and recording details.	26
To develop children's skills at interpreting large-scale maps and aerial photographs.	3f. *Making and using maps: Level B.*	Comparing an aerial photograph and a large-scale map, both of an area known to the children.	Photograph/map interpretation.	29
Mapping				
To improve basic mapping skills by encouraging the making of maps of imaginary places.	3d *Making and using maps: Level B.*	Designing a map of an imaginary Antarctic town.	Map-drawing activity and discussion.	32
To distinguish between side views and plan views of everyday classroom items.	3d. *As above.*	Relating side and plan views of common classroom objects.	Playing 'Snap' and matching games.	33
To begin to make simple maps of a classroom using colour as a key.	3d. *As above.*	Making large-scale maps of the classroom for a reason.	Arranging and sticking furniture on large-scale map. Reporting to other children.	35

GEOGRAPHY KS1

Learning objective	PoS/AO	Content	Type of activity	Page
To begin to make simple maps of places the children know well.	3d. *Making and using maps: Level B.*	Adding details to a map of the school.	Fieldwork in school grounds. Individual or paired mapping work.	37
To show details on maps or plans in picture form or by using symbols.	3d. *As above.*	Using symbols to represent routes and landmarks around school.	Fieldwork in school grounds. Route-making/ map-making work.	39
To establish that maps and plans at different scales show varying amounts of detail and information.	3e. *Making and using maps: Level C.*	Recognising different scales using maps of a farm.	Worksheet and discussion for pairs or small groups.	41
To help children recognise that different scales of maps exist and that maps of different scales will have different characteristics.	3e. *As above.*	Comparing maps at different scales using a viewfinder window.	Individual examination and comparison of maps.	43
To recognise that the globe and world map show the same information but in different ways.	3e. *As above: Level B.*	Making a simple world map and comparing with globe.	Paired tracing, cutting and sticking.	45
To ensure that children know that the UK is made up of four constituent countries which, with the Republic of Ireland, make the British Isles.	3e. *As above.*	Making a model of the British Isles. Locating and naming constituent countries.	Small group, papier-mâché model-making.	47
To enable children to mark where they live on maps of their country and area.	3e. *As above.*	Drawing own homes and locating them on local and UK maps.	Individual drawing and contributing to class display.	49
To provide an opportunity for children to make a map or plan of their own classroom and use it to identify simple routes.	3e. *As above.*	Making and comparing routes around the classroom.	Individual or paired route-making, drawing and map-making.	51
To follow a route from a simple map.	3e. *As above.*	Designing and following routes.	Paired route-designing in the hall or playground. Following routes set by others.	53
Studying your locality				
To recognise the school locality as being the immediate vicinity of the school, the area that children know well.	4. *Physical and built environment: Level A.*	Walking around the school locality to determine its bounds.	Fieldwork. Small group walks in school's locality.	56
To recognise the school locality's main physical features.	5a. *As above.*	Identifying physical features in the school locality.	Fieldwork. Small group walks or brainstorming using worksheet.	58
To recognise the school locality's main human features.	5a. *Recording and presenting: Level B.*	Collecting and sorting evidence on human features.	Fieldwork. Small group walks in local area. Sorting and displaying evidence.	60

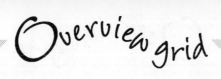

Learning objective	PoS/AO	Content	Type of activity	Page
To recognise that a locality has its own character which is the result of its human and physical features.	5a. *Place and people's effect on each other: Level B.*	Selecting describing words for a locality and drawing it.	Individual worksheet-based work.	61
To consider the positive physical and human characteristics of your locality.	5a. *As above.*	Identification of key physical and human features in the locality.	Individual work on banner design.	63
To help children understand that the clothes we wear reflect the weather conditions.	5c. *As above: Level A.*	Sorting and explaining clothing for different weather conditions.	Group collecting and sorting activity.	65
To relate the weather to people and their surroundings using a story context.	5c. *As above.*	Recording weather and linking it with people's lives.	Individual weather recording and creation of cartoon-style weather story.	67
To develop an awareness of how the weather affects local people and their surroundings.	5c. *Place and people's effect on each other: Level A.*	Identifying indoor and outdoor leisure facilities.	Paired map interpretation and colouring.	69
To partake in a decision-making process as to how a piece of land could be used.	5d. *Making and using maps: Level B.*	Designing a potential children's play area.	Field sketching in the school grounds. Map-based design work.	71
To recognise the many ways in which land and buildings are used in your local area.	5d. *As above.*	Recording land and building use in the local area.	Fieldwork – drawing and modelling local buildings.	73
To recognise that other places will have some things the same and some things different from your locality.	5b. *Physical and built environment: Level B.*	Sorting places according to similarities and differences.	Group picture-sorting exercise. Cutting and sticking.	75

Studying other localities

Learning objective	PoS/AO	Content	Type of activity	Page
To understand that everyone lives in their own locality, an area which they regard as home.	4. *Physical and built environment: Level B.*	Using a wide range of evidence to learn about a locality.	Collecting, sorting and displaying resources.	78
To recognise the physical features of a contrasting locality.	5a. *As above.*	Recognising physical features of another locality.	Individual worksheet activity. Drawing selected physical features.	80
To recognise the human features of a contrasting locality.	5a. *Place and people's effect on each other: Level B.*	Features and routes in another locality.	Drawing places and routes as a paired game.	82
To be able to question what it is about a locality that gives it its character.	5a. *As above.*	Identifying the character of another locality by designing a postcard.	Individual postcard design. Worksheet drawing and writing activity.	83

GEOGRAPHY KS1

Learning objective	PoS/AO	Content	Type of activity	Page
To consider how the weather affects a contrasting locality and the people who live there.	5c. *Place and people's effect on each other: Level B.*	Considering the weather in another locality and its effects.	Pairs or fours presenting a weather forecast.	85
To be aware that land and buildings are used in ways which are characteristic of their locality.	5d. *As above.*	Identifying details of buildings and land in a contrasting locality.	Paired model-making based on map interpretation.	87
When children learn about another locality they will notice some similarities and some differences between it and their own.	5b. *As above.*	Recognising similar and different characteristics.	Individual worksheet activity to write descriptive poems.	89
Studying environmental quality				
To learn that environments have attractive and unattractive features and that views on such features differ.	6a. *As above.*	Ordering their drawings of places in the school according to their likes and dislikes.	Paired drawing around school grounds. Group discussion.	92
To appreciate that environments change, sometimes for the better, sometimes for the worse.	6b. *As above: Level C.*	Enquiry about issues of change in school or locality.	Fieldwork in school grounds. Rôle play in newspaper office, creating a newspaper.	93
To recognise that the quality of an environment can be sustained and improved.	6c. *As above.*	Identifying the quality of features around the school grounds.	Walk around school grounds and group model-making.	95

Entries given in italics relate to the Scottish 5–14 Guidelines on Environmental Studies (Social Subjects: Understanding people and place).

Early geographical skills

The activities in this section of the book aim to develop skills which children will need if they are to operate successfully as geographers.

They should be able to:
▲ use geographical vocabulary;
▲ begin to undertake fieldwork activity;
▲ follow directions;
▲ gather information from secondary sources.

Mapping skills are covered separately in the next chapter.

The National Curriculum divides geography into three component parts: skills, places and geographical themes, but the subject should be taught in such a way that children are using geographical skills to study themes in the context of places. Different geographical skills are necessary and relevant to all areas of geography.

In their geographical work children should be provided with opportunities to observe, question, record and to communicate ideas and information. The activities in this section encourage enquiry and practical activity. Whenever possible the work is related to the children's own locality, with particular emphasis being laid on the school and its grounds.

Working through this section will ensure that the children have covered geographical skills within Key Stage 1. In addition, each activity has a thematic angle and could be used to support thematic work of various sorts. Work on places is also covered.

 EXPLORE YOUR SCHOOL

To encourage children to explore their own surroundings.

†† *Pairs within a group.*

🕐 *20 minutes for group discussion; 15 minutes for sketching around school; 15 minutes for further discussion.*

⚠ *Make sure that children are aware of the places within school where they are and are not allowed to go.*

Key background information

In the early stages of their geographical development children need to be encouraged to explore purely for the enjoyment of exploring and then to talk about their discoveries. The child's 'discoveries' must always be given value so that the child knows that it is 'all right to look for yourself'.

Preparation

Spend some time exploring the school buildings and grounds yourself. Prepare a simple sketch of a place within the school that all the children will recognise (perhaps the cloakroom or the entrance hall). Keep your sketch technically simple and expect the children to have a little laugh at your expense when they first see it.

Resources needed

Your own sketch, a large stock of drawing paper, pencils (coloured pencils if desired), a copy of photocopiable page 102 for each pair.

What to do

Sit the group around you and show them your sketch. Encourage a little humour as it is important to limit any worries that the children may have about doing sketches of their own and then sharing them.

Ask the children:

▲ Where was my sketch done?

▲ How do you know?

▲ What things in the picture helped you decide?

▲ Have I left anything out of the sketch?

It is then worth asking whether you could have added anything else to your sketch to make recognition easier (colour, for example, or information about smells or sounds).

Show the children one of the photocopied sheets and tell them that they are going to get into pairs and have a walk around the school grounds. Emphasise where they are allowed to go and where they are not. If necessary, adults or older pupils could be asked to supervise younger children.

Tell the children that they should spend at least ten minutes exploring, then they should choose a place to sketch. To avoid children seeing each other sketching pairs could be sent out one at a time, while the rest of the group gets on with other activities. Once back in the classroom the children should improve the detail of their sketches and fill in their names in the top, left-hand box.

When all the pictures are complete they should be displayed for the whole group to see. Each pair in turn then challenges another pair to identify the place they drew. Encourage discussion to check the children's awareness of the school environment.

Suggestion(s) for extension

If you have a large-scale plan of the school the children could make their own display by arranging their pictures around the plan and then linking them to the relevant places with lengths of thread.

The idea of each place having smells, sounds, textures, or even associations with taste can be developed. Children who write confidently could be encouraged to produce written descriptions, or even poems, to describe a place which others then must guess.

Suggestion(s) for support

To avoid dithering, each pair could be given a secret location once a period of exploration has taken place.

Pair the children so that one confident sketcher accompanies a less confident one.

Assessment opportunities

Photocopiable page 102 allows the children to record who guessed the location shown in each sketch. The real assessment opportunity is at the second discussion stage when children are reporting back on their walks around the school and showing their knowledge of the school by identifying each other's sketches. This should enable you to decide whether individual children are beginning to show an ability in the simplest of fieldwork skills, those of observation and communication of findings. Are children able to ask:

▲ Where is...?

▲ What is it like at...?

Opportunities for IT

Children could use a word processor to write a simple description of their sketched picture. They could decide what fonts to use and how large the font should be if the labels are to be read from a distance as part of a class display. Alternatively a class book could be made from all of the pictures and their descriptions.

If the school has a scanner the sketches could be used within a word-processing package.

Display ideas

If the children display their sketches around a large-scale plan of the school, linking the sketches to their locations on the plan with thread, this will create a child-generated display feature. An interactive version of this might include some photographs taken around the school. Children could then be asked to fill in a form from a pile at the side of the display

indicating where they think each photographed location is. Photograph numbers and location names could be supplied on the form so that children only need to link each correct pair by drawing a line.

Other aspects of the Geography PoS covered

Geographical skills – 3b, f.

Reference to photocopiable sheet

The children can use page 102 to do their sketch. In addition they write in their own names, both as artists, and on the sketch that they identified. They can use any space at the bottom to write describing words for their location. This provides assessment of how the children use geographical terms in exploring their surroundings.

THE WORDS WE USE

To help children become familiar with geographical vocabulary.

†† *Small group.*

🕐 *30 minutes.*

Previous skills/knowledge needed

The children will need some experience in playing simple word games and card games like 'Snap'.

Key background information

It is important to encourage a broad and exciting use of geographical language within the classroom and during field activities. However, it is equally important that children should not be put off by unnecessary jargon.

Always start with the vocabulary that the children are already using. The main thing is that they can tell you that the playground is 'messy' or 'dirty' – terms like 'pollution' can come later. Once the understanding is there the teacher can use the odd technical term. On occasions it might be worthwhile congratulating a child who uses a more technical word and using the opportunity to teach the true meaning of this new word to the rest of the class.

Early geographical skills

Preparation

Talk to the children about the different words that they might use in connection with the work you are covering. Use pictures, posters or materials relating to your work to support your discussion. Take copies of photocopiable page 103 so that each member of the group can have one. Provide a selection of pictures connected with your topic (more than there are children in the group).

Resources needed

A copy of photocopiable page 103 for each member of the group, card, scissors.

What to do

Ask each child to select one picture from those you have provided. Give each child the photocopied sheet and ask them to cut out the words. (These will be more durable if stuck on to A4 card before cutting up.

The children should then place (or stick) any words they think relevant on to the appropriate parts of their picture. For example, if a child has a picture of a snow-covered mountain with a cable car passing over a conifer forest she might place 'above' on the cable car and 'below' on the forest.

Children could then move on to select two images which contrast with each other (perhaps a city street in the UK and a city street in India). Discussion can come from the children's decisions about which labels are relevant to which pictures.

The word cards could also be placed in relevant places around the classroom.

Suggestion(s) for extension

These activities can lead into writing activities with valuable discussion about exciting sentence construction. Artwork can also be used to extend the activity.

Suggestion(s) for support

Pair a more able child with a less able, particularly with respect to reading.

It is possible to tackle the activity in a very different way by showing a short piece of documentary-style video about a place and asking the children to 'shout' out any words from the list as, and when, they feel they are relevant. This obviously involves some risk, in terms of noise and excitement, but can be very rewarding. This approach can support children who are struggling with their reading and give them a little extra confidence.

Assessment opportunities

If children have successfully stuck words in suitable places the pictures could be kept as evidence that children are using and understanding geographical terms.

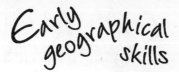

Opportunities for IT

The children could write their own pairs of positional or directional words using a word processor. They could then print these out and stick them on to their pictures.

To help provide a range of contrasts and environments, pictures for this activity could be taken from a suitable CD-ROM. The children could also select the pictures they wish to use from a library of pictures from the CD-ROM. With assistance children could place their chosen pictures into a suitable word-processing package and add words or sentences next to the picture.

Display ideas

The finished pictures could be used for a group display. Alternatively, children could make a class picture (possibly in connection with topic work or a story they have heard) suggesting positional, directional, comparative and evaluative words which could be added to the picture on labels. An interactive version of this display could have word labels which must be matched to various word positions on the picture. Children would know they had succeeded when a word 'fits' the other half of its 'jigsawed' label.

Other aspects of the Geography PoS covered

Geographical skills – 3c.
Places – 5a.
Thematic study – 6a.

Reference to photocopiable sheet

Photocopiable page 103 provides a selection of words which the children can use to label pictures or the classroom. Some of the words are positional, some directional, some comparative and some evaluative. This sheet could be enlarged on a photocopier to make each label larger, the pages could also be glued on to card before the children cut out the words.

BIG PLACES – LITTLE PLACES

To encourage an awareness that places are of different sizes and are referred to by different geographical terms.

†† *Class split into three groups.*

🕐 *More than one session.*

Previous skills/knowledge needed

The skills required include cutting, sticking and model painting – it would be helpful if children have had some experience of box modelling before.

Key background information

It is important that young children begin to understand that we live in settlements, and that these may range from a single isolated house to a large city. They should also learn that settlements of different sizes are described by different terms such as 'village,' 'town' and 'city'.

Modern settlements are often extremely complex, they overlap each other until it becomes hard to judge what particular 'type' of settlement you are in. This is further complicated by the way that one size of settlement can contain other smaller sizes of settlement. Children should be aware of the terminology so that they can begin to learn about settlements.

Preparation

Make a collection of small card boxes, such as those used in food packaging, and equipment necessary for cutting and sticking these. Prepare a modelling area, remembering to provide protection for tables, floor and children's clothing. Collect a number of pictures of villages, towns and cities and the buildings in them.

Resources needed

Three card or plywood base boards (approximately 80cm square), a selection of old card packaging suitable for box modelling, glue, scissors, painting materials, picture resources of different sizes of settlements.

What to do

Put the children into three groups of different sizes. The smallest group will make a model village, the middle group will make a model town and the largest group will make a model city.

Show the children the collection of picture resources on different settlements and discuss the building and activities they can see in the pictures. Ask the children if they can tell you which pictures are of large places and which are of smaller places. Can they tell you which pictures show villages, and which show towns and cities? Can they describe any

Assessment opportunities

Assess children's understanding that places can be different sizes, as well as their ability to use geographical vocabulary. Concentrate on individuals in follow-up discussion or listen to children's talk during the model-making activity. Photocopiable page 104 can be used to assess children's recognition of words connected to settlement and their ability to sort them according to settlement type.

Opportunities for IT

Children could use a simple desk-top publishing package with a page divided into three columns; 'village', 'town' and 'city'. They could then work in groups to type in words which represent the types of buildings found in each settlement. This activity could also be set up using a simple spreadsheet to provide the columns.

Children could also use framework software like *My World 2* with the *Town and Village* resources file to design and build their own town or village. This is done on the computer screen by dragging different types of buildings on to a grid of streets.

differences between a city and a town? Aim to establish that towns are bigger than villages, and that cities are bigger than towns.

Show the children the three base boards and explain that they are going to build a model of each of the three sizes of settlement. Explain that the city model should cover the whole of one of the base boards, so therefore the town will cover only the middle part of its base board and the village only the very centre. Draw circles on the town and village base boards to show the area which should be 'built' on. The three groups could work simultaneously, or one group could work at a time. Each child chooses a building which she thinks would typically exist in the settlement type she is working on and makes her own little model of that building. The groups then position their buildings on the base boards and finally stick them in place.

Once all the houses are completed and stuck in place the three finished models can be painted.

Suggestion(s) for extension

Some children may be more capable of grouping buildings according to their type and size. Challenge these children to place the buildings appropriately within the circles.

Suggestion(s) for support

Video tape which shows villages, towns and cities will support children in their understanding of the differences between these types of settlement. Children should realise that settlements come in different sizes and should become familiar with the relevant geographical vocabulary. Make sure that less able children attempt to model simpler, less detailed buildings.

Display ideas

The three finished models will make excellent table-top displays, particularly if the children have painted them. It is important that the spare base board area around the outside of the town and the even greater space around the village are painted to show that they are, for instance, farmland. A wall behind the display could be used to display pictures of villages, towns and cities – group pictures of each type of

Different places		
Name:		Date:
village	town	city

▲ Copy these words in to the correct columns.
Some words might go in more than one column.

market square · railway · flats · town hall · superstore · post office · cinema · park · station · pond · cottage · trees

▲ Add your own words if you can.

settlement behind the appropriate model and use appropriate words to label the display. Computer spreadsheets or completed copies of photocopiable page 104 could also be displayed.

Other aspects of the Geography PoS covered

Geographical skills – 3e, f.

Places – 4.

Thematic study – 5a, b.

Reference to photocopiable sheet

Photocopiable page 104 challenges the children to decide on words which are appropriate to each type of settlement. Words are selected from the bottom of the sheet and written into the relevant column. It is important to emphasise that some of the words could be placed in more than one column.

FOLLOWING A ROUTE

We can follow directions to find a route or place.

†† *Two pairs at a time.*

🕐 *40 minutes.*

Previous skills/knowledge needed

Children will need to be familiar with the geographical vocabulary necessary to be able to follow and give directions.

Key background information

Children must begin to develop the language skills needed to understand geographical directions if they are to be able to give directions themselves.

They need to understand the concept that compass directions are constant ('north' is always north). Children will be using 'left', 'right', 'north', 'south', 'east' and 'west', as well as language like 'face', 'move' and 'turn'.

Preparation

Set out nine markers and compass direction arrows as shown in the illustration. Label the markers 1–9.

If you are working on a field the arrows and their direction labels might be pegged or weighed down to stop them blowing away. If working on a playground they might be chalked on the tarmac.

The distance between each marker is not important although children enjoy the activity more if they have a little distance to run.

Resources needed

You will require nine markers (such as cones or PE stands), north, south, east and west arrows written on card and labels with the numbers 1 to 9 for the markers. Each pair will need a copy of photocopiable page 105. You will also need at least one compass to help set the activity out.

What to do

Select two pairs of children. One pair will design a route and the other will follow it. The pairs can then swap over.

The children will gain valuable experience if they are involved in correctly aligning first the north arrow, then the other arrows, using a compass. Take time to explain how a compass works, and that north is always north.

The first pair of children design a route around the nine markers, starting from the middle and visiting each marker only once. They draw the route they have designed on their copy of photocopiable page 105 using lines and arrows. They then give their route to the other pair.

One child from the second pair starts at the central marker and prepares to follow the route, making a note of the numbers of the markers she visits, in order. Her partner describes the route by referring to the original pair's plan – using the terminology 'north', 'south', 'east' and 'west' as appropriate. The original pair watch to make sure the route is followed correctly.

The pairs can then swap roles and repeat this activity.

Suggestion(s) for extension

Encourage children to write their directions out long hand as this will prompt them to use an even wider range of directional and positional vocabulary.

Another possible extension of this activity is for children to be blindfolded, then directed around the route by a caller.

Suggestion(s) for support

Demonstrate the activity to less able children and reduce the number of markers to aid the less confident.

Visually handicapped children can also enjoy this activity if directions are called out to them by sighted children.

Assessment opportunities

Note the level of ability the children show following the route.

An interesting extension is to make a large floor grid divided into squares which are the same distance apart as the floor robot's unit of movement (30cm for a ROAMER). Each square could contain a different picture. Children can then take it in turns to program the robot to move around the grid to the chosen square.

Alternatively children can set up their own obstacle course and challenge each other to direct the floor robot around the course. Children should also begin to record their directions so that another child can come along and check that the directions given are correct.

Display ideas
Make a small model version of the nine markers as an interactive table-top display. Provide a stack of blank copies of photocopiable page 105 for the children to use.

Other aspects of the Geography PoS covered
Geographical skills – 2; 3e.

Reference to photocopiable sheet
Photocopiable page 105 is a plan view of the activity, used by one pair to plan the route, then by the other pair to follow the route.

Opportunities for IT
Children could use a floor turtle, linked directly to the computer or a ROAMER or PIPP programmable floor robot to develop these skills further.

They can start with a positional language of backwards and forwards, left and right, but will need to be introduced to compass points as they progress. Stickers could be placed over the turn arrows on the floor robots to help them understand the points of the compass.

🌳 PICTURE TRAIL

To develop fieldwork skills within the school's locality.
†† *Small groups.*
🕐 *20 minutes for discussion; 30 minutes for fieldwork; 15 minutes for follow-up.*
⚠ *If you are going outside the school grounds you may need extra adult helpers.*

Previous skills/knowledge needed
The children will find this activity easier if they are used to sketching and drawing outdoors.

Key background information
Children's fieldwork skills should be developed from an early age. The easiest place to do this is in their own school locality (one of the localities which should be studied under Place in the programme of study). This includes the school buildings and grounds, and any surroundings which are easily accessible.

In this activity the children have to make a 'view trail'. This involves structured observation, recording and communication in the field and helps develop the children's understanding of their local area.

Preparation
Make one copy of photocopiable page 106 for each child. You will need a large-scale map of the area around your

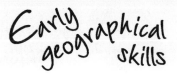

school for use in the discussion and follow-up parts of the activity. A large version of the photocopiable page could be used in the introductory discussion. Prepare to take the children out of school in small groups – arrange extra adult help and inform parents of your intentions.

Resources needed
One copy of photocopiable page 106 for each child, a supply of clipboards, pencils, rubbers and pencil sharpeners.

What to do
Explain to the children that they are going to go on a walk around the school area, and that you want them to record this walk so that a friend can later follow their route. They will do this by drawing pictures of different parts of their walk. At this point you could use an enlarged version of photocopiable page 106 which shows a walk round the school building. Encourage the children to draw the view of the direction they are going to walk in, walk to the furthest point of that view, then draw the next view and so on. They will end up with a series of pictures which lead the viewer through the route. Show the first group a large-scale map of the school's locality and let them choose the route they will follow. Routes must be reasonably short as the children will need some time at each drawing site.

Make sure the children understand what is required, then let them set off on their walk under the supervision of an adult. As the group leaves the school grounds, each child draws a view of the direction that they are going to walk. This is drawn in the first of the six boxes on the photocopiable sheet. The group then agrees on the next place to stop. This should be the furthest place on their route shown in the first drawing. Once at this place the children draw the new view in the second box on their worksheet. This is repeated until all of the six boxes are filled in.

Once the walks are completed, groups can join together and challenge each other to describe each other's routes from the drawings. Alternatively, children from different groups can join in pairs and describe their partner's route.

This activity develops the simple, but useful, geographical skill of field sketching so it is worth emphasising the benefits of accurate and careful sketching, particularly to more able

pupils. Check the children understand that it is more important to include key features than lots of detail.

Suggestion(s) for extension
The activity could be given a thematic angle by sending the children on a route which lends itself to identifying and sketching different types of houses, different forms of vegetation or different transport features. Children would then be working to the parts of the Programme of Study which refer to *human* and *physical* features. One effective way of doing this is to ask the children to sketch their views in pencil and to colour, for example, only the transport features.

Suggestion(s) for support
Make sure that the groups are kept fairly small and check that the adult accompanying each group understands what is expected. More able children could be used to support the less able.

Assessment opportunities
If the children work in small groups this provides an excellent assessment opportunity. The accompanying adult can be given a list of children's names so that they can record which children are able to correctly sketch the views and which realise where the next sketching point might be each time.

Opportunities for IT
A good alternative to the children sketching their views is for them to use a camera to make a 'photo trail' of the route. Children's routes can be displayed in the same style as the worksheet or on the classroom wall.

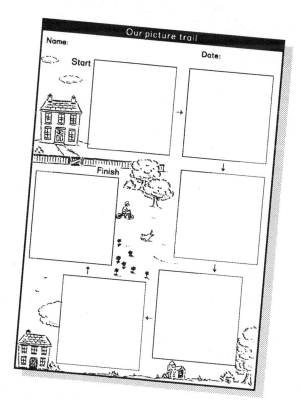

TAKE A GOOD LOOK

To observe and record school surroundings. To use fieldwork skills to create a database about the school buildings and grounds.

†† *Whole class split into four groups.*

🕒 *40–60 minutes.*

Once photographs have been taken, either by the children or teacher, the best ones can be placed on to a Kodak CD ROM (this can be done by taking the relevant pictures to a branch of Boots the Chemist). The pictures can then be viewed and used on the computer so that the children can add pictures to an electronic trail.

Pictures can be put into a word processor with children adding simple text to explain the picture. Older or more able children might be able to make a trail guide, taking perhaps just six pictures and making a small leaflet giving details of their six locations.

Display ideas

The large-scale map of the school and surrounding area could be displayed on the classroom wall with the routes children took marked on it. The completed photocopiable sheets could then be placed around the map with lengths of thread linking each page to the route it shows.

If a camera is available, photos of the routes could also form an interesting display. This could be made interactive if the photographs have Velcro on the back and patches of Velcro for them to be stuck to position in a line on the wall. Challenge the children to put the photographs in the correct order.

Other aspects of the Geography PoS covered

Geographical skills – 3a, c, e.
Places – 5a.

Reference to photocopiable sheet

Photocopiable page 106 provides six boxes which can be filled with sketches of views on the children's route.

Previous skills/knowledge needed

This activity asks the children to complete a simple table, so previous experience of this kind will be useful.

Key background information

Children must be given opportunities to observe, question what they see, record systematically and communicate their findings. Quality geography stems from these basic skills.

This activity will emphasise that the children can easily create a simple system to access a wealth of highly relevant, interesting and useful data. Once created, a database can be used in many different ways.

Preparation

Explain to the children that a database is any organised collection of information from which data (information) can easily be deposited or withdrawn. Discuss any databases that they might already be aware of – perhaps their school file or medical records. Start a brainstorming session where children come up with ideas on what might be included in a database for their class (or school). What types or categories of information would be of use in future topics or areas of work? (It is worth giving this some thought yourself before tackling the problem with the class.)

Resources needed

Paper and clipboards (or something for the children to press on), pencils and other drawing equipment, copies of photocopiable pages 107 and 108.

What to do

Discuss your school buildings with the children and try to decide on four 'sides' to your school buildings. If your site is a complicated one it may be easier to choose one particular building.

Organise the children in four groups, each group having responsibility for one 'side' of the school.

Ask them to draw a simple sketch of their side of the school and to show on their sketches all the details below:
▲ all the external windows;
▲ all the external doors;
▲ all the chimneys;
▲ where the drains and downpipes are;
▲ the design and angles of the roof;
▲ the building materials used.
   Photocopiable page 107 could be used for this.

Drawing should be encouraged as a form of recording because it stimulates a high quality of observation if taught carefully. Make sure that the children recognise the need for accuracy. Encourage the children to:

▲ look at the shapes of the building;

▲ look at the materials used;

▲ look for different colours.

When the groups have completed their drawings of each side of the school building the class can come together to discuss their findings and fill in a data collection sheet (photocopiable page 108 may be used). Encourage the children to use a structured system for drawing together the information from all their drawings. Explain that this will make the information more useful and interesting.

Photocopiable page 108 could be enlarged so that the whole class can see it, or the children could fill in individual copies with some support.

Children could be asked to record their findings in a written format or alternatively they could use an audio tape recorder, or with support, a video camera.

Suggestion(s) for extension

Greater detail could be used in this activity, with children being asked to record, for example, information on window frame materials, door materials, parts of the building which are newer or have been modified, or details like air bricks or fire alarm boxes.

An excellent follow-on is to build a model of the building, making sure that it has all the correct features.

Children can be asked to write down which time of the day their side of the building gets the sun.

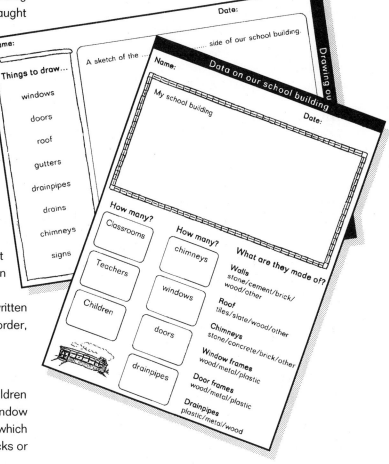

Suggestion(s) for support

If your building is a complex one, you could sketch the outline of each aspect of the building before photocopying the sheets for the children. Bear in mind that a group of children will all be drawing the same side of the building, so it will not greatly matter if one child concentrates on drawing a small part of the building in great detail while neglecting the rest.

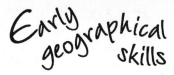
Assessment opportunities

The drawings can be retained as evidence of each child's ability to observe and record information from the environment. Photocopiable page 108 can only be used for assessment if the children complete them individually using the drawings as a secondary source.

Opportunities for IT

Cameras, video cameras and tape recorders can be used as information technology solutions to gathering evidence. Indeed if the children start using these within the school grounds this will lead to more informed and skilled usage in other places as the children get older.

Children could also use an art or drawing package to make their own pictures of the sides of the school. The use of a drawing package would enable them to make shapes of different sizes, then stretch and move them around the screen (such as rectangles for windows and doors). They could learn how to fill shapes with colour and position them in the correct place on the screen. Many drawing packages have a 'click to grid' option which automatically lines up different parts of the drawing or ensures that straight lines are actually horizontal and not at a slight angle.

Children could also use graphing software to record some of the data they have collected, perhaps the number of windows or doors on each side of the school. Alternatively the information could be entered into a simple computer database so that children can search or sort the information to ask questions such as:

▲ Which side has the most windows?
▲ How many windows are there altogether?

Display ideas

Display the collection of children's drawings with a selection of their completed database forms. Local buildings may be happy to supply items such as a brick, a slate and a piece of downpipe. These will enhance the display and make it more tactile.

A three-dimensional model of the building would provide an excellent focus for the whole display.

Other aspects of the Geography PoS covered

Geographical skills – 3f.
Places – 4; 5a, d.
Thematic study – 6a.

Reference to photocopiable sheets

Photocopiable page 107 provides a structured way to observe and record information on the school building. Page 108 can be used to bring all the various pieces of information together into a database. This might then be used in other work at a later date.

KEEPING THE TRAFFIC MOVING

To provide children with simple fieldwork data collection skills.

†† *Pairs within a group.*

🕐 *10 minutes for the introduction; 15 minutes for fieldwork per pair; 20 minutes for the group conclusion.*

Previous skills/knowledge needed

Children should be capable of a short period of work away from the teacher and classroom. The activity involves some basic counting and recording of information on a simple worksheet.

Key background information

Children should be introduced to the fieldwork skills involved in a simple survey at an early age. This activity introduces the children to the idea that a number of surveyors can go out to collect data and that the data collected can then be combined to provide a larger 'picture'. This simple and safe school-based activity teaches the children about traffic flows in terms of people moving about a building and provides them with skills which prove useful in similar, more advanced fieldwork when they are older.

Preparation

You will need to obtain or draw a simple large-scale plan of your school which shows the main internal walls, doorways and corridors in the building. Some of the main places could be labelled to help the children get their bearings.

Decide on how you are going to group the children and then choose three or four sampling points around the school building (one point for each pair in a group). Select sampling points which will have very different numbers of people passing. Mark these sampling points on the large-scale map.

Make enough copies of photocopiable page 109 so that each child can have one copy.

Resources needed
A large-scale plan of the school buildings, one copy of photocopiable page 109 for each child, clipboards, pencils.

What to do
Talk to the children as a group about the plan of the school buildings (if they are new to this suggest that the roof has been taken off the buildings so that someone hovering in a helicopter can look down and see inside). Ask if they can identify different places on the plan.

Discuss with the children the problems of congestion in busy corridors. Ask if they can guess which parts of school are the busiest and which are the least busy. Then explain that they are going to find out about this.

Show the children a copy of photocopiable page 109 and explain that they will go, in pairs, to one of the sample points on the map and write down how many people pass that sample point during an agreed period of time, possibly by using a simple tally system.

The children are unlikely to be adept at time keeping and may not have the means to do so. Provide each pair with a five-minute sand timer, or with a watch or clock marked with the start and finish positions of the minute hand. If these options are not possible other children could act as starter/finish 'runners' from the classroom.

Send each pair of children to their sample point and ask them to count the number of people who pass that point during the agreed period of time. Five, or possibly ten minutes is usually enough time. They then write the number in the relevant place on their sheet.

When the children return to class, the group (or whole class if each group has carried out the activity) compare their 'traffic' counts. The children compare their findings to discover which sample points are the busiest and least busy – they then draw pictures of these two places in the relevant boxes on the photocopiable sheet. They should also write a sentence to say *why* they think the places are busy or not busy.

Suggestion(s) for extension
This activity could be extended by asking groups of children to sample the same points at different times during the school day. They might find that different locations are busy at different times. They might also realise that certain places have 'rush hours' when there is suddenly a lot of traffic. More able children may think of reasons why certain places are busier than others and could suggest how 'traffic flows' could be improved (perhaps by moving furniture from corridors).

Suggestions(s) for support
Children who have problems with concentration are best paired with a friend who will support them. It is worth talking to even quite young children about counting methods such as the tallying system.

25

Assessment opportunities

The best opportunity for assessing children's data collecting and interpreting skills is when they are reporting back to the rest of their group or class. The sentences written on the photocopiable page can be used as evidence of individual children's understanding of the outcome of the activity.

Opportunities for IT

The data collected by the survey can be dealt with in several ways. Children could use simple graphing software to record and plot the results from the traffic surveys, either at the same point at different times of the day, or different points at the same time of day. The results can be shown either as block graphs or pie charts.

An alternative would be to create a simple database with a record for each place where the traffic flow data is collected. The record could be set up like this:

Place	Main Entrance
9.00	20
10.00	5
11.00	3
12.00	16
1.00	22

Children could then search and sort the database to find answers to questions such as:
▲ What is the busiest time in the school?
▲ Which place has the least traffic at 9.00am?

Display ideas

A wall display of the plan of the school showing the sample points could be labelled with the names or pictures of children who collected data at each site.

Graphs (possibly computer generated) or tally charts could be displayed around the map, also the sheets with the children's completed pictures and sentences.

Other aspects of the Geography PoS covered

Geographical skills – 2; 3e.
Places – 5d.
Thematic study – 6c.

Reference to photocopiable sheet

Photocopiable page 109 can be used by children to record the number of people who pass a sampling point in their school buildings. A number of groups of children will all be using copies of this sheet to collect data. Once the group or class has data on a number of sample points the busiest and least busy places can be identified by the children and drawn in the appropriate boxes. They are also asked to write a sentence suggesting why these two places are the busiest and least busy.

SECONDARY SOURCES

To use sources other than first-hand experience to obtain geographical information.
†† *Pairs within a group.*
🕐 *40 minutes or more.*

Previous skills/knowledge needed

It will help if children are used to playing different rôles, they also need to be able to read the names of local roads and complete a simple sheet with information collected from estate agents' details.

Some previous work on local large-scale maps may be of benefit, and a little introductory work on why people move house and how an estate agent helps them.

Key background information

Children should understand that they already use a wide range of secondary sources. They use non-fiction books in class, watch television, and many are very capable at using computers.

This activity encourages children to use a new type of secondary source, estate agents' house details.

Children will become aware that piles of paper full of information are very cumbersome and that the information becomes much easier to handle when it has been 'interrogated' and the relevant details are highlighted. This introduces really valuable research skills.

Preparation

Gather a selection of estate agents' house sales details from your school's local area. Try to obtain a range of details from different agents for varying sizes and types of property and make sure that the details have photographs of the properties fixed to them. Aim to have at least twice as many details as you have children in the group.

Take a copy of photocopiable page 110 for each child.

If possible, turn the rôle-play area into an estate agency – a pad of paper, a telephone, a typewriter (or better still the class computer with a word-processing program operating), an old or toy camera and some sign boards and posters (which the children could design and make) would all make excellent 'props'.

Resources needed

A collection of pictures and posters showing different types of house, a supply of estate agents' details with photographs attached, a range of items to create an estate agency rôle-play area in the classroom, copies of photocopiable page 110.

What to do

Talk with the children about why people move house (need for more space as a family grows, job move, and so on) and why such people use estate agents. Some children may have moved house themselves. Discuss what they like about their houses and what they don't like. Use the collection of pictures of houses to stimulate these discussions.

Let the children explore the estate agency in the rôle-play area and discuss what the daily routine of an estate agent might be.

Tell the children that they are going to pretend that they are looking for a house. They will need to decide whether they want a new or an old house, whether it should have a garden and how many bedrooms they need. Let each pair of children visit the estate agency and fill in their copy of the photocopiable sheet as they sort through the details that you have collected. You could pin these to the wall just as they would be in a real estate agency.

By filling in the photocopiable sheet the children are 'interrogating' secondary sources and making informed decisions based on what they see.

Worthwhile discussion can follow this activity. Encourage the children to use geographical vocabulary, including terms such as 'detached' and 'semi-detached'. Promote the idea that a house has to meet certain criteria, but that these will be different for different people.

Use the photographs on the front of the details to stimulate discussion, and possibly written follow-up work, on which of the houses each child likes best and why. This will challenge the children to make judgements about the quality of the environment and their likes and dislikes.

Suggestion(s) for extension

The children could make their criteria for a house more complex (should it have a garage, a downstairs toilet and so on). They could design their own more complicated version of photocopiable page 110 for this purpose. They could also make estate agents' details for their own houses.

Children could 'sell' houses to each other, using some of the details in the rôle-play area. This would give more able children a chance to show their ideas to the rest of the class.

Suggestion(s) for support

If children have problems locating the information they need you could go through the details first and highlight the information that they will be searching for with a highlighter pen.

Assessment opportunities

Copies of photocopiable page 110 will provide evidence of how well the children interrogate secondary sources. Any follow-up work on their likes and dislikes when selecting houses from the details could provide evidence on their expression of views on the attractive and unattractive features of an environment (PoS 6a).

Opportunities for IT

Children could input some simple house details into a database set up in advance by the teacher, or they could create their own database. In either case children should have opportunities to use the database to answer such questions as:
▲ How many houses are detached?
▲ Which house has the largest number of rooms?
or more complex questions such as:
▲ How many houses have a double garage and are in the town?
▲ Which houses have double glazing and gas central heating?

If the children are to set up their own database they will need to spend some time in group or class discussions about

27

the headings (fieldnames) in the database. They will also need to decide how to classify information such as the size of garden, or the location. Gardens might be classified as: none, patio, small, medium, large.

It is helpful to create a data collection sheet which gives children a limited number of choices so that they must use one of them to describe a feature. This aids consistency and makes the database easier to use. It is also a good idea to make sure that children collect the data in the same order that they will enter it into the computer.

Once children have collected their data they might work in pairs, or with the support of an older child or other adult, to type in their data. If they work in pairs one child should check the work of the other child, both for keying errors and for mistakes in the data itself. Extra spaces or full stops can often cause havoc with searches!

The database might contain the following fields:

Location	town/country/city etc
Rooms	7
Bedrooms	4
Type	detached, semi detached, terrace etc.
Garage	none, 1, 2 etc
Garden	large, small etc
Features	GCH, DG

Some databases have tokenised fields so that children can only select from the offered choices which are set up in advance. This makes entry and later searching much more consistent and reliable.

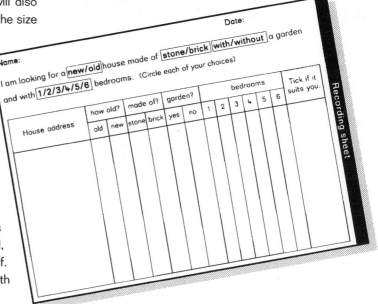

Once the children start to search they will need to be introduced to facilities such as simple searches, sorts and printing out their answers in tables or even graphs. Leave plenty of time for this activity so that children really have time to use the database and do not just enter their information.

Children could write their own descriptions of a house, using estate agent language. This could be done using a word processor or simple desk-top publishing package. A standard page could be created in advance, giving spaces or frames for pictures, main details and a room-by-room explanation. Alternatively this could be reduced to just a single front page giving the key features of the house, picture and price.

Children could also use an art package to draw house facades. These could be used to illustrate their own sets of estate agent details.

Display ideas
The children's completed photocopiable sheets could be displayed as part of the estate agency rôle-play area along with the original details and any details which the children have made for their own homes.

Children could design and make a sign for the agency and 'for sale' boards to use in rôle-play.

Other aspects of the Geography PoS covered
Places – 5a, d.
Thematic study – 6a.

Reference to photocopiable sheet
Photocopiable page 110 is an information recording sheet for children sorting through estate agents' details. They will be able to fit the details of several houses – and will end up with ticks against the houses which fit their chosen criteria.

THE VIEW FROM ABOVE

To develop children's skills at interpreting large-scale maps and aerial photographs.

†† *Pairs.*

🕐 *30 minutes.*

Previous skills/knowledge needed

Children should have undergone simple work on the plan view or looking down on things from above.

Key background information

The ability to read and interpret large-scale plans and maps is a very important one. Aerial photographs can help children's understanding of maps as well as developing their ability at using photographs as a source of information.

Aerial photographs are a very valuable resource as they allow detailed interpretation of an area and, like maps, they can show patterns and distributions. This activity encourages comparison of large-scale maps and aerial photographs of the same area.

Try to have both vertical and oblique aerial photographs of your own school. These should, if possible, be in colour.

Preparation

You will need one or more aerial photographs of your school or somewhere the children know well. If you do not already have such photographs, try your local secondary school, your local advisor or inspector, your local planning department or a commercial provider such as those which advertise widely in geographical and educational periodicals.

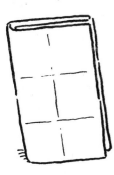

You will also need a large-scale map covering the same area. This should be a fairly representational map such as the 1:1250, 1:2500 or 1:10000 scales produced by the Ordnance Survey – avoid local street plans which often have the widths of roads exaggerated and contain too much writing. Each pair will require one copy of photocopiable page 111 and an A4 photocopy of the part of the map which shows the same area as the photograph.

Choose five or six features shown on the vertical aerial photograph that are also shown on the map and colour each of the features a different colour. Features such as a prominent park, a school, an area of woodland, a river or a tower block would suit well.

Resources needed

Aerial photographs of your school locality or an area known to the children (colour vertical photographs if possible), one or more large-scale maps (Ordnance Survey) covering the same area, A4 photocopies as described above.

What to do

You can introduce the activity to the children as a class, in groups or in pairs, but the activity itself is best carried out in pairs.

Show the children the vertical aerial photograph and the large-scale map and let each pair have a period of time to look at them and get used to them. You could introduce the map and photograph in a group context and start off by playing a simple game with the children celebrating their ability to match items in front of their friends.

In their pairs, the children take one of the prepared photocopies and try to locate the map features that have been coloured in on the photograph. They then fill in photocopiable page 111 by drawing the feature as it appears on the map in the first column and as it looks on the photograph in the second column. They write the name of the feature in the last column.

Suggestion(s) for extension

Children who complete the task quickly could go on to colour in other features on the map photocopies and complete a second copy of the photocopiable sheet. In doing this they will be identifying prominent features as part of a cross-referencing process.

Most local authorities have a licensing agreement with Ordnance Survey which allows them to provide schools with computer forms of local maps. This would enable the school to have computer versions of the area around the school which can then be edited and printed out to make very large-scale maps of small areas.

Display ideas

An effective wall display can be made by displaying children's maps and completed worksheets around the aerial photograph. Mapped features and photographed features could be linked by string or wool. If you wanted this display to be interactive you could attach just one end of each piece of string or wool and invite children to link them with the correct map or photograph feature. You could even label the features with letters and numbers and get the children to write which letter goes with which number. The answers could be provided on a 'lift-the-flap' piece of card on the display.

Other aspects of the Geography PoS covered

Geographical skills – 3a, e.
Places – 4.
Thematic study – 5a.

Reference to photocopiable sheet

Children fill the photocopiable sheet (page 111) with details of the features they have identified.

Suggestion(s) for support

Write the names of the features you have coloured in on workcards or on the board to provide less able children with a little more confidence in locating the features on the photograph. This will also provide them with the words for copy writing. Use workcards if you wish to differentiate the activity, as the more able children will still have to provide the words from their own vocabulary and will not have the written help in identifying the features.

Assessment opportunities

Completed copies of the photocopiable sheet will provide summative evidence of the children's ability at using these secondary sources. To provide hard evidence of their ability the children could perform the aerial photograph, photocopied map and photocopiable sheet part of the activity in isolation. Asking the children to report back their findings to a group or class discussion at the end would provide an opportunity to make notes on each child's individual understanding.

Opportunities for IT

Talk with the children about the technology involved in obtaining aerial photographs. The children can play with toy or model aeroplanes, flying them over map-style floor mats and pretending that the pilot is taking photographs from an aerial camera. Apart from the benefits in reinforcing the idea of map-making from the sky as a technological solution to a mapping problem, this will also reinforce the idea of the plan-view.

Many CD-ROM packages are now available with aerial views of localities. If you have a scanner, it may be possible to scan in an aerial photograph and get the children to edit the duplicated images of it. If good-quality photographs are available these can be put on to a Kodak CD-ROM for use in the classroom.

Looking down from the sky

Name:

Date:

1 map view	2 photograph view	3 name of feature

▲ Look at the map and the aerial photograph.
▲ Copy the features on the map in the first column.
▲ Copy the features on the photograph in the second column.
▲ Write the name of the feature in the third column.

Mapping

Children must be able to make and use maps with confidence. This whole section is devoted to teaching children the skills related to making and using maps.

Activities involve the children in:

▲ making maps and plans of real and imaginary places;

▲ using pictures and symbols in making maps and plans;

▲ appreciating the meaning and relevance of scale;

▲ identifying major geographical features on both globes and maps;

▲ locating and naming the constituent countries of the UK;

▲ using maps to show where they live;

▲ following a route on a map.

These mapping activities will also be relevant to work on geographical themes and the study of places. Children may have to undertake work out of the classroom, perhaps studying their local area.

The children should have access at all times to at least one globe and one map of the world within the classroom. Obtain or make a large-scale map of your school's locality – this resource will prove very valuable as it can be used in many different ways. It is also worth developing a collection of maps of different sorts, particularly ones connected with your own locality and any other localities you study.

ALL IN THE MIND!

To improve basic mapping skills by encouraging the making of maps of imaginary places.

†† *Individuals.*

🕐 *Up to one hour.*

Previous skills/knowledge needed

Any work which encourages children to think and draw creatively will be useful preparation for this sort of activity.

Key background information

Several key components to mapping can all be encouraged through imaginary map activities. The plan view, application of scale, symbolisation and use of a key, aligning by direction and reference by using coordinates can all be approached in this way.

In this activity children are asked to plan a modern town for Antarctica. This provides them with a useful starting point.

Teachers can use this activity as a diagnostic exercise to check how children's mapping skills are developing. They can also use it to encourage children to demonstrate skills they have already developed.

Preparation

Spend some time discussing what it is like in Antarctica:
▲ What type of buildings do you think you would need to live there?
▲ What type of vehicle would be best suited to such a place?
▲ What kinds of jobs would people have?
▲ Which leisure activities might be possible?

Some pictures of the Antarctic would help the children understand what the place is like. Show them where it is on the globe.

It would be very worthwhile to involve the children in discussion about how the Antarctic is presently a protected environment under international treaty.

Provide the children with large sheets of paper to draw their maps.

Resources needed

A globe and pictures of the Antarctic, pencils and pencil crayons, or a large sheet of paper for each child.

What to do

Make sure that the children have a good grasp of what it is like in Antarctica.

Explain that virtually all the continent is covered with thick ice and discuss the problems which the extreme cold can create, especially in winter and at night.

Ask the children to design a town for Antarctica, specifying that their design must be in map form.

If you are using this exercise for diagnostic reasons decide how much discussion there should be about what makes a good map. It can be an interesting exercise to leave the children completely to their own devices, then use the results as stimulus for discussion on how the maps could be improved.

Encourage the children to be creative in their imaginary mapping then, at the discussion stage, compare individuals' maps as regards clarity, detail, and whether they have used symbols, keys, the plan view or some form of clearly identified scale.

Set a time limit to prevent children getting carried away with adding detail.

When the maps are finished spend some time asking the children to explain their designs. This can provide a valuable insight into how they see the mechanics of mapmaking.

Suggestion(s) for extension

Children who produce maps with a clear plan view and use some symbols should be encouraged to produce keys. To extend the activity still further ask children to draw a simple

grid over their map and to devise a locational system using letter and number coordinates.

Poetry and creative writing will follow on neatly from this exercise, as will descriptive writing about their imagined towns.

A locality study on an Antarctic research settlement could be researched and linked with work on the history of exploration and the quest for the South Pole.

Suggestion(s) for support

This activity can be tackled by children of all abilities but some may need help to get started. Provide a list of places which could be included: houses, school, hospital, harbour, helicopter landing pad and so on.

Encourage the children to use pencil for their first draft as they are likely to change their minds a good deal. Once the outline design is completed crayons can be introduced.

Assessment opportunities

If used diagnostically the finished maps can be kept to illustrate the children's developing mapping skills. A check list might include the following:
▲ Is the design obviously in plan view?
▲ Are details drawn in pictorial fashion?
▲ Are details in plan view form?
▲ Are some details shown in symbol form?
▲ If symbols have been used, is there a key?
▲ Has any attempt been made to show scale?
▲ Has an attempt been made to show direction?
▲ Has a grid system been used?

A similar activity could be set later in the year to see if any of these conventions are more firmly in place.

Opportunities for IT

Children could use CD-ROM atlas or encyclopaedia materials to look at images and maps of Antarctica. They could also use a drawing package to create simple maps of designs for their own towns.

Framework software like *My World 2* and the *Geography Key Stage 1* resources could also be used to develop children's understanding in this area.

Display ideas

The finished maps could be used as a wall display around a map of Antarctica and with a globe nearby. The class could vote on their favourite map from the class and a larger wall picture, possibly in collage form, could be created with the different parts of the town labelled.

Other aspects of the Geography PoS covered

Geographical skills – 3a, e, f.
Places – 4; 5a, b, c, d.
Thematic study – 6c.

SIDE VIEW – PLAN VIEW

To distinguish between side views and plan views of everyday classroom items.
†† *Small groups.*
🕐 *10–20 minutes.*

Previous skills/knowledge needed

Children should be able to play a simple 'snap' game.

Key background information

One of the most important skills in using and making maps concerns the individual's ability to recognise the perspective, or the view point, of a map. Maps tend to view the area they represent from above, an unfamiliar viewpoint for most children.

Children should be encouraged to develop this ability through games like those suggested in this activity. They need to understand that many things look very different when seen from above and that it is the plan view which is shown on maps.

Preparation

This activity requires lengthy preparation by the teacher, but once prepared can be used many times by children who can quickly become self-supporting at it.

Resources needed

A camera capable of photographing small items in close up. A flash facility on the camera would be useful.

What to do

Choose either 12 or 18 items from around your classroom and/or school. These should all be quite different in shape when viewed from the side and from above. Items which are

particularly suitable include the following:
- ▲ water pot;
- ▲ container with scissors in;
- ▲ globe;
- ▲ book;
- ▲ cotton reel;
- ▲ 3-D maths shapes;
- ▲ sitting Teddy bear;
- ▲ play telephone.

Photograph each of these items in close up from the side and from directly above, focusing the camera correctly. The side views are best taken with the object standing on a table and the camera on the same level as the centre of the object. The top views are best taken with the objects on the floor and the photographer standing over them (be careful to avoid photographing your toes!).

Once the film has been developed it is a good idea to protect the photographs so that they will survive repeated use by the children. This is best done by laminating or encapsulating them. Consider having more than one set of prints developed as there are various applications for the pictures.

Small groups of children can play 'Snap' with the finished set of pictures by sharing the shuffled pile of 24 or 36 pictures, then taking it in turn to place a card face up. Whenever a card is placed which follows its own alternative view, the first to call 'Snap' picks up the pile and adds it to their hand. The winner is the last child with cards left.

The cards can also be used in matching games where children are encouraged to match each plan view with its side view. One version of this is to lay all the photographs out face down, then let the children, one by one, turn over two cards. When two cards are revealed which go together, the child keeps them. If the cards do not go together they must be turned over again. The game becomes a memory

game as children try to remember the location of cards they have already seen.

Photocopiable page 112 can be used to provide evidence that children can match a side view with its plan.

Suggestion(s) for extension

Children who are adept at matching these views of classroom objects should begin to depict the objects in drawn plan form. Challenge the children to match the photographs, identify the plan view, then draw the plan view of the object. By using the top view photograph children will begin to appreciate what can be seen in a plan view and what is hidden. One good example of this is the globe, as a plan view of this does not show the base.

Suggestion(s) for support

It is important to photograph a range of objects from your classroom and school. Make sure that some of these objects are easy to identify from above (perhaps a globe or a Teddy bear). Children who have difficulty understanding the plan view often benefit from standing over the real object to confirm the photograph.

Assessment opportunities

'Snap' and matching games provide excellent opportunities for the teacher to observe groups and individuals as children often become quite engrossed in what they are doing. Use this opportunity to record how individuals cope with the idea of the plan view.

Opportunities for IT

Talk to the children about the role of the camera in this activity. They could also be involved in the choice of objects and in taking the photographs.

Photographs could later be scanned into a computer format or put on to a Kodak CD-ROM so that they can be used in slide show programs on the computer. Children could then use a word processor to write a narrative for each picture, experimenting with the layout of text and picture on the page and the size and style of font used. A concept keyboard, linked to a word processor, could also be used for children to match side and plan view of the same object.

An alternative activity would be to use simple multi-media authoring software which allows children to enter pictures

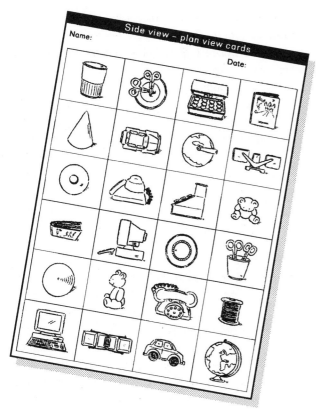

CLASSROOM MAPS

To begin to make simple maps of a classroom using colour as a key.

†† *Groups within a class.*

⏱ *15 minutes for group activity; 5 minutes for class discussion; 15 minutes for further group activity; 10 minutes for class discussion.*

Previous skills/knowledge needed

Children will need to be able to work cooperatively within a group. They will also need to be able to use adhesive. They should also be familiar with recognising the 'plan view'.

Key background information

Young children should begin to develop their spatial ability as early as possible. They should begin to get experience of using the plan view and arranging things in space. In this activity the children are supported as they come to terms with a very large-scale map and are then encouraged to create their own new map of their classroom. The activity asks the children to use colour to represent different features in the classroom and so leads into the skill of making a key.

Preparation

Prepare a large, very simple sugar paper plan of your classroom for each group. Draw the outline of the classroom, leaving a gap for the door and marking the position of any windows. Then, from other colours of sugar paper, cut out shapes for the carpet, lino, tables, tray-units, computer table, storage units, shelving units and display units in the room. These should all be simple rectangle, square or half-hexagon shapes and should be in scale to your base plan. Each type of furniture should be a different colour and you should prepare the exact number of each item that will be needed to 'furnish' the plans accurately.

If you are using photocopiable page 113 as follow up to this activity you will need to make a copy for each child.

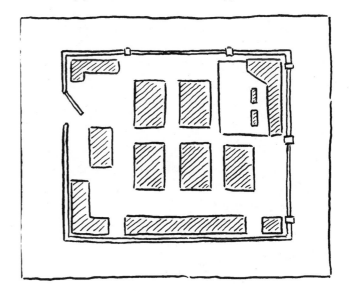

and text but to also record their own voices, then use this as a commentary to the photographs. Such packages allow different pages to be linked in an interactive style. The software could be used to set up a quiz for children to identify the objects either from the plan or oblique view.

Display ideas

If you have a spare set of pictures, shape each set of two so that they fit together to make a two piece jigsaw. Try to make each pair unique in its joining pattern. This can be done by slightly overlapping each set of two pictures and then cutting through both of them to make a joining shape.

Mount each top view image on thick display card, then mount the side view images on the wall within easy reach. The children have to match the pictures backed on to card with the pictures mounted on the wall. The unique join between each pair confirms that the children have matched the pictures correctly.

Other aspects of the Geography PoS covered

1b.

Geographical skills – 2; 3a, f.

Reference to photocopiable sheet

Photocopiable page 112 can be used to reinforce the matching of side view to plan view. The sheet contains twelve side views and twelve plan views of objects found in school. The pictures are arranged at random on the sheet but can be coloured, cut out, matched and then stuck on to backing paper.

Mapping

rearrange the class furniture they can be allowed to stick it in place. Each group can then take it in turn to report their suggestions to the rest of the class, using the plan they have created.

The logical, although brave, next step is to let the children vote for the plan they like best, then rearrange the furniture to match this plan.

An optional follow on to the re-designed maps is to ask the children to decide where they would all sit in the theoretical new classroom and then to draw their most common journeys on the plan. If all the children do this you will end up with a 'traffic-flow' map as the children will have identified the busiest walkways between the furniture. At this stage they might choose to make these busier routes a little wider. Photocopiable page 113 can be used as a follow on to this activity. It gives children an opportunity to design the internal layout of a classroom, using a simple colour key.

Resources needed
Sugar paper classroom plans and sugar paper furniture plan views, adhesive for sticking paper, copies of photocopiable page 113 for follow up.

What to do
The groups can work at the same time, thus making this a class activity, or you can work with each group separately, bringing the children together for class discussion. Modify your instructions accordingly.

Bring the class or group together and show them one of the large-scale outline plans that you have prepared. Discuss which corner of the classroom is which. The children will find it easier to orientate the map by looking at where you have placed the doors and windows.

Explain that each group is going to be given a set of paper plan view furniture for the room and that this furniture is in scale and relates to the real furniture that is in the room.

Each group works collaboratively to place the paper furniture in the correct places in the room. Children could be encouraged to measure relative distances, perhaps by pacing. When a group is finished, stop the rest of the class and gather them around the table so that everyone can see the plan. Discuss with the children whether the group have positioned the furniture correctly. If the groups are all working at the same time then the class should look at each finished plan one at a time. The furniture should not be stuck down at this stage.

Now gather the class together again and ask them whether they like the way the classroom is arranged. Discuss alternative arrangements for the furniture. Give individuals a chance to make suggestions and then justify them.

Now send the children back to their groups and ask them to rearrange the paper furniture. It is worth making the point that they need to work together.

Once each group has agreed on how they would like to

Suggestion(s) for extension
If children complete this activity quickly you could ask them to include greater detail on their plans. More able children could try the same activity for the school hall or library area. They could draw the room plan themselves and decide on the paper colour for any items of furniture or PE apparatus. Individuals may recognise the need for a key to show what each of the colours means. Encourage them to design a key for their group's plan.

Suggestion(s) for support
Group the children to ensure that less able children are supported in their work. It might actually benefit such children if the group sizes were smaller.

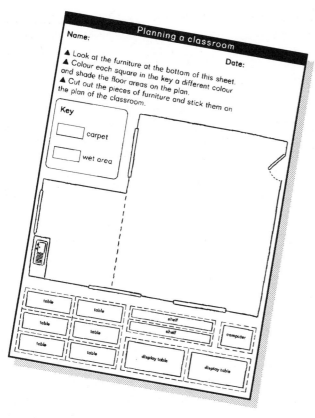

Planning a classroom

Name:

Date:

▲ Look at the furniture at the bottom of this sheet.
▲ Colour each square in the key a different colour and shade the floor areas on the plan.
▲ Cut out the pieces of furniture and stick them on the plan of the classroom.

Key

[ ] carpet

[ ] wet area

table | table
table | table | shelf
table | table | shelf | computer
table | table | display table | display table

with the plan they will be ready for use when the plan is loaded. Children could then be shown how to copy or duplicate these shapes and drag them into their new positions. Any spare or unused items can be deleted once the final plan has been drawn.

Display ideas

Display the finished plans, using as a centrepiece the plan that the class selected as the one they would like to adopt. The display will be particularly effective if children have made large colour keys which can be displayed alongside their plans.

Other aspects of the Geography PoS covered

Geographical skills – 3c.

Places – 5d.

Thematic study – 6a, b, c.

Reference to photocopiable sheet

This activity can be extended by asking children to complete photocopiable page 113. It shows a plan of an imaginary classroom with a carpeted area, a wet area and a sink already marked. Children colour in the key and the corresponding area. They then cut out the furniture and arrange it on the classroom plan.

If children have problems understanding which piece of real furniture matches each one on their plans you could put coloured stickers on the tables, chairs and so on to assist children in matching their sugar paper furniture to the real furniture in the room.

Assessment opportunities

The best opportunities for assessment are as the children are preparing their maps or when individuals are speaking at the reporting stage.

Photocopiable page 113 can be used to provide evidence that individuals understand and can use these map-making skills and are also capable of recognising how a simple colour key works.

Opportunities for IT

At the planning stage of the re-designed classrooms children could use a drawing package to assist them in the design of the classroom. The teacher could provide a basic room plan, saving it to disk so that groups of children can use the plan as the basis for their own design. They could use the box or rectangle drawing tools to draw and position different items of furniture in the room. They could also be shown how to fill the shapes with colour to identify different pieces of furniture. Older children could even add a colour key for identification purposes using text commands as well.

To make the task easier the teacher could pre-draw a set of different objects for children, drawn to scale and arranged on the edge of the original plan. If these are saved along

LET'S MAKE A MAP!

To begin to make simple maps of places the children know well.

†† *Individual or pairs within a group.*

🕐 *30–40 minutes.*

Previous skills/knowledge needed

Some previous work with symbols would be useful but is not essential.

The children should be familiar with the part of the school building in which they are based.

They should be beginning to draw simple maps and be able to explain them. These early maps will be little different from pictures which show where things are.

Key background information

This activity encourages children to prove that they can understand the plan view and it teaches them to use simple symbols. The activity also relies on the children recognising that a simple map is a scaled-down version of reality. Play activities with models will have established within children the idea that we can work at scales smaller than the real world.

Preparation

Make a very simple large-scale plan of the school building in which your class is based. There might already be a base plan available. If this is not totally accurate its 'shortcomings'

Mapping

can be a useful starting point for discussion with the children.

All the plan needs to show is the main walls, with gaps representing the external and internal doorways. Any permanent, structural features could be included to give the children a few points of reference (items such as islands of cloakroom pegs, for example).

Make enough copies of photocopiable pages 114 and 115 so that each child may have a copy.

Resources needed

The large-scale simple map of the school building, a copy of photocopiable pages 114 and 115 for each child, a supply of colouring pencils.

What to do

Display the large-scale plan where all of the children are able to see it.

Discuss the plan with the children and get them to orientate it (decide which way up it is). In this group situation use the more able children to involve the less able in working out which corner is which, which doorway is which, and so on.

Give each child a copy of photocopiable page 114 and talk to them about the symbols used in the key. Explain that they have to copy the plan on to their worksheet and then copy the symbols provided in the key on to the correct places on their plan.

The children may well find the activity easier if they are allowed to walk around the school building. This should be encouraged as it will develop the skill of orientating the plan and will help the children to really get to know and understand the plan.

Suggestion(s) for extension

If the children seem to have understood the concepts involved, and have enjoyed the activity, one extension could ask the children to start with the blank photocopiable sheet, this time using the symbols to redesign the internal layout within the existing classroom walls.

A further extension would be to ask the children to devise their own symbols for things not included on the photocopiable sheet.

Once the paper activities are completed a model of the mapped area could be built using a construction kit such as LEGO.

Photocopiable page 115 allows children to demonstrate how clearly they understand the plan view and using symbols. They simply re-draw the bedroom scene as a plan and create symbols for the specified items.

Suggestion(s) for support

If children find it difficult to copy the large plan on to their photocopiable sheets, you could draw your original at A4 size and photocopy it on to the photocopiable sheet before the activity begins.

It would be possible to start with the modelling idea

Mapping a bedroom

Name: Date:

Look at this picture of a bedroom.

▲ Draw a plan of the room in the space below.

Name: Date:

A map of my school building

Mapping our school building

Key

books

computer

water

sand

dressing up

art

coats

PE

38

(suggested as an extension activity). Starting with a three-dimensional model may help children to understand the plan as they can look down on the model and see the school as it would look like from above with the roof removed.

If the jump to symbols is too great, let the children draw purely pictorial maps. Less-confident children might prefer to work in pairs.

Assessment opportunities

The completed photocopiable sheets will give some evidence of whether children are capable of making maps and plans of real places using pictures and symbols. Better evidence will be gained by extending the activity so that the children are drawing their own maps from scratch.

Photocopiable page 115 provides an opportunity to find out whether the children can translate a sideways view into a plan view and whether they can use appropriate symbols in the correct context.

Opportunities for IT

Maps of the school or classroom could be prepared in advance using a mapping or drawing program and saved on to a disk for use by the children. They could be printed out and used as a base map for children to add their own items, or colour different areas. Older or more able children could add furniture to a classroom plan by drawing rectangles and placing them on to the class map at the appropriate point. This would encourage them to use simple drawing tools, re-size objects and then drag them to the correct places on the plan or map. Children could also add colour to the different objects they have drawn. The final maps could be printed out and used for display purposes.

Younger children could also use framework software like *My World 2* and suitable resource files to achieve similar results.

Display ideas

Some of the copies of photocopiable pages 114 and 115 could be displayed around your original large-scale plan. Any models made of the building could be displayed on a table in front. Photographs of various locations within the building could surround the display with lengths of wool connecting them to their locations on the plans. The children could copy out larger versions of the symbols they have designed and these could be included in the display.

Other aspects of the Geography PoS covered

Geographical skills – 3b.

Places – 4.

Reference to photocopiable sheets

Photocopiable page 114 provides children with support as they design real maps of their own school. The sheet supplies them with simple symbols which they must add to a copied plan of their school building. Photocopiable page 115 can be used as follow up and is designed to reinforce the idea of using symbols and transferring an oblique view to a plan view.

PICTURES AND SYMBOLS

To show details on maps or plans in picture form or by using symbols.

†† *Individuals or pairs within a group.*

🕐 *25 minutes for route following/map making; 15 minutes for discussion; 25 minutes for map making.*

Previous skills/knowledge needed

Children will need to understand what a route is. They also need to know which parts of the school they may visit.

Key background information

Children need to deal with the problem of how to record detail on a map or plan. Young children will solve this by drawing items of detail in picture form, but the more experience children have of making and using maps, the earlier they will master the slightly more abstract solution of inventing symbols and drawing keys.

Preparation

Think of a number of locations around the school buildings and grounds. Group these locations into pairs so that to walk from one place to the other a child would have to follow a simple route which has some easily identifiable 'landmarks'.

39

Gather together a small number of everyday objects from the classroom for use in introducing the second half of the activity. Ensure a good supply of large pieces of paper and prepare copies of photocopiable page 116 for extension work.

Resources needed

Several everyday objects from the classroom, at least two large pieces of paper per child (some children might want to use several).

What to do

First of all, tell the children that they are going to draw a map of a route around the school. Discuss the meaning of the word 'route'.

Let each child or pair choose one of the routes that you worked out in your preparation (it may be easier to have less able children attempting shorter routes).

Ask the children to walk their routes and then draw a sketch map of it. Make sure they understand that they must draw any 'landmarks' or items of detail that they come across in the relevant places on their maps. When the children have completed this part of the activity encourage them to show their maps to each other and to talk everyone through their routes. The problems involved in having to draw detailed items on their routes should be highlighted in this discussion. Praise children who have drawn landmark items in plan form.

Next, show the children a selection of everyday items from the classroom. Some will be easy to draw but others will be inappropriate to draw in a representative way on a map. Agree on some symbols which could be used for these objects (perhaps a simple light bulb sign instead of a lamp or a circle containing the letter 'g' instead of a globe).

Ensure that all of the children realise what a sign or a symbol is. Now ask the children to redraw their maps, making up symbols for 'landmarks'. Keep reminding them that a symbol does not necessarily have to look like the real thing but that it does have to be simple and clear.

In conclusion bring the children together, asking them to show both their maps and tell how they changed the pictures to symbols.

Some children may wish to rewalk their route during the second phase of the activity.

Children may realise that they need to make a key for their symbols. This is a very encouraging development and can be a starting point for further discussion.

Suggestion(s) for extension

Children can design keys for their maps, bearing in mind that the real test of the quality of their symbols is to see if another person can tell them all apart.

Ask the children to draw another route, using the same symbols and key as before. A child who can do this successfully will quickly realise that published maps, like those of the Ordnance Survey, use the same symbols on all their series of maps.

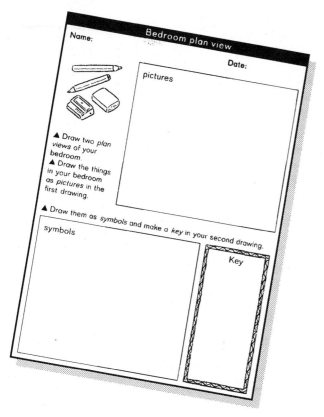

or school, adding symbols that they have designed using the software. Children need to be shown how to use the 'cut and paste' or 'copy/duplicate' commands of the software so that when they have drawn their symbol they can simply reproduce it as many times as they need and place it at the appropriate place. They could also use copies of the symbols to make a key. This would involve adding text to the drawing.

Display ideas
The completed maps can make an attractive display. To make this interactive children could choose their most successful symbol and draw both the picture, and its symbol form, on pieces of card. These could then be mixed up on a table in front of the display and classmates could be challenged to match pictures to symbols.

A three-way version of this display is to have a side view drawing, a plan view and a symbol form of each item.

Other aspects of the Geography PoS covered
Geographical skills – 2; 3a.
Places – 4.

Reference to photocopiable sheet
Photocopiable page 116 can be used either in the classroom or at home to reinforce the idea that symbols can be used to show where things are on a map.

The children are asked to draw their own bedroom in plan form, once as pictures and once with symbols and a key.

Photocopiable page 116 asks children to draw two plans of their own bedroom, one with items of detail in picture form, the other with them in symbol form with a key. This could be used to reinforce the skills learned in this activity.

Suggestion(s) for support
A less confident child could be given a shorter or more straightforward route. Children could also be paired so that a more confident child supports a less confident one.

If children find it very difficult to come up with symbols for objects you could suggest they use small circles containing the initial letter of the object.

Consider allowing the children to use colour as this makes the whole activity more fun and provides a wider range of symbol possibilities.

Assessment opportunities
The finished maps will provide evidence of each child's ability at working pictorially or symbolically in mapping. The children will need to complete these individually if they are to be used as evidence for assessment.

Opportunities for IT
Maps of the school or classroom could be prepared in advance using a mapping or drawing program and saved on to a disk for use by the children. Children could design their own simple symbols using a drawing package and add them to the maps of the class.

Older or more able children could also use the drawing package themselves to create their own maps of the class

WHERE ON THE FARM?

To establish that maps and plans at different scales show varying amounts of detail and information.

†† *Pairs within a small group.*

⏱ *30–40 minutes.*

Previous skills/knowledge needed
Children will find this activity easier if they have already undertaken some work using plan views. This can be done by getting the children to look down on objects in the classroom. Model buildings, particularly a model farmyard, could be used very effectively in preparation.

Some simple reading and writing skills, also cutting and sticking skills, will be needed for this activity.

Key background information
Children must begin to recognise that maps and plans depict information at various scales. The activity tackles this concept by using four maps of the same farm, each drawn at a different scale.

Children should begin to understand that something can be drawn large or small and that if the same item is drawn smaller on the same size of paper as before, then more

Mapping

surrounding detail can be included. On the other hand, if the item is drawn bigger on the same size of paper, more detail within the item can be recorded. The former we call smaller scale, the latter larger scale.

Preparation

Children will each need a copy of photocopiable page 117 and a large piece of backing paper on which to stick the different sections of the photocopiable sheet.

Set out the materials that the children will need.

Resources needed

Glue, a pair of scissors for each child, some drawing materials, pieces of backing paper a little larger than A4, a copy of photocopiable page 117 for each pupil.

What to do

Talk to the children about what a plan view is and about what we use maps for. Discuss with them how it is possible to draw 'close ups' of things, or make them very small in drawings. Introduce them to the idea of maps at different scales.

Show them photocopiable page 117 and spend some time reinforcing the idea that each of the four maps shows the same farm. Asking the children to colour the maps may be time-consuming but could be worthwhile if it helps the children to differentiate what is what on the maps. Tell the children to cut out the four maps and the four sentences, then match each sentence to the correct picture. Ask the children to arrange the maps in order, with the smallest-scale map first and the largest-scale map last. You could tell them that as they go from one map to the next it should look like they are getting closer and closer to the farmhouse.

The children can then draw lines on the maps to identify the routes described in the sentences.

As a follow-up piece of work it would be very valuable to involve the children in using maps of varying scale of their own school. Show the children a 1:25 000 map and a larger

scale (say 1:10 000) map of the school and ask them about the differences in detail. (This would be particularly effective if you folded the maps so that their paper area was the same.)

Suggestion(s) for extension

The farm maps, once arranged and glued, can lead to creative writing. The children could tell a story about the farm and the horses who live there, referring to the maps as they do so.

Suggestion(s) for support

Less able and more able readers could be paired up. Discussion between partners is often beneficial to both.

If the sentence matching and route work is too demanding for some children, limit the exercise to cutting out and ordering the maps.

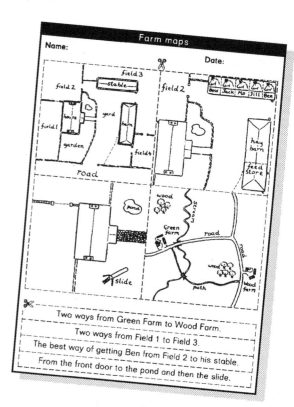

Reference to photocopiable sheet

Photocopiable page 117 is essential to this activity. It asks the children to order maps according to scale and to decide which map is most appropriate for showing routes of varying length and detail.

ALL AT DIFFERENT SCALES

To help children recognise that different scales of maps exist and that maps of different scales will have different characteristics.

⁛ *Individuals.*

🕐 *15–25 minutes.*

Previous skills/knowledge needed

Some knowledge of what a map is will be useful, although this activity could be used to introduce mapping. Children will need to be able to fill in a tick table.

Key background information

Maps are effectively a means of communicating information. They are created for all sorts of different reasons and the scale is chosen to suit the person who is going to use the map.

Work like this can help young children as they begin to understand how small places fit within larger places (districts within towns, towns within countries and so on).

Assessment opportunities

Children will provide evidence of ability at using maps at different scales if they complete the activity without help.

Photocopiable page 117 could be used to assess this. Sit with each child in turn and ask him to point to the map which 'shows the greatest real area on the ground' or which 'shows the most information about the house itself'. Alternatively, provide each child with the four maps already cut out and ask them to order them while you watch.

Opportunities for IT

Talk with the children about real maps, showing them some published maps and asking them how they think the maps are made. Hopefully the children will begin to understand the role of information technology in the making of modern maps, as well as the rôle of vertical air photography and computer drawing systems. If possible compare a vertical air photograph with a map of the same place so that the children begin to appreciate how many modern maps are generated.

Display ideas

Display the finished ordered maps, along with any creative writing they have inspired.

One way to reinforce the activity through display is to enlarge a copy of each map and then draw a box on each depicting the bounds of the next map in order.

Other aspects of the Geography PoS covered

Geographical skills – 3d.

Preparation

Make a collection of globes, plans and maps of different types and scales. Any will do, but try to include within the collection some maps which the children might recognise (perhaps a local 1:50 000 Ordnance Survey Landranger sheet or a local A–Z).

Some other possibilities include:

▲ world wall map
▲ globe(s)
▲ a map of Europe
▲ road atlas
▲ motoring maps
▲ walking maps
▲ local maps
▲ plans of the school
▲ builder's plans
▲ kitchen design lay-out plans.

GEOGRAPHY KS1

Display these maps and plans on a wall, folding them so that at least an A4 section of each is on view. Label each map with a short title.

Make copies of photocopiable page 118.

Resources needed
One copy of photocopiable page 118 for each child, maps, plans and globes displayed so that they are accessible to the children.

What to do
Talk to the children about scale and the fact that globes, and some maps, have to cover very large areas of land and sea. Explain that we call maps like these 'small scale' because everything on them has to be much smaller than it really is.

Give each child a copy of photocopiable page 118 and ask them to cut the bottom section off. They should then cut out the rectangle in this section to end up with a frame containing a 'window' which is 6cm by 9cm. This 'window frame' will help them to examine each map.

Ask the children to choose four maps to look at and show them how to place the window over parts of each map in turn. They can then fill in the table on the upper half of the worksheet by ticking if they can see a particular feature through the window as they visit each map. The activity works best if children decide where on each map they are going to position their window and refer only to what they can see within it as they fill in the table.

Suggestion(s) for extension
Once the children have filled in their photocopiable sheets ask them to identify which of the four maps they looked at uses the largest scale and which has the smallest scale.

Map window				
Name:				
Date:				
	map 1	map 2	map 3	map 4
the whole world				
whole continents				
seas				
whole countries				
cities as dots				
roads as lines				
villages				
woods				
rivers as lines				
buildings as rectangles				
roads and streets				
buildings in detail				
walls and fences				
trees on their own				
house doorways				
car parking places				

cut this out and look through the window

If the children wish to go further you could label each map on display with its scale in the form of... '1cm on the map = ... on the ground'.

Common examples would be:

▲	1:10 000	1cm on the map = 100m on the ground
▲	1:15 840 (A–Z)	1cm on the map = 158m on the ground
▲	1:25 000	1cm on the map = 250m on the ground
▲	1:50 000	1cm on the map = 500m on the ground
▲	1:100 000	1cm on the map = 1km on the ground
▲	1:190 080 (3 mile:1")	1 cm on the map = 1.9km on the ground
▲	1:300 000	1cm on the map = 3km on the ground
▲	1:3 000 000	1cm on the map = 30km on the ground

This would help the children to appreciate what scale really means.

Suggestion(s) for support
If children find the basic map interrogation difficult reduce the number of maps, or provide just four maps of the same place, such as a map of Europe, a British Isles map, a 1:50 000 map and a local map such as an A–Z.

Children will also find the activity easier if you dispense with the 'windows' from their sheets and simply affix your own permanent window to your chosen area of each map.

Assessment opportunities
At the end of the activity each child should have a completed photocopiable sheet. You could then ask children, individually, to show you their sheet and tell you which map they visited was a large-scale map, which a small-scale map and why. This would provide evidence that each child was capable of using maps, plans and globes at a variety of scales.

Opportunities for IT

You may be able to borrow or buy a computer map package which shows maps of different scales. Your local planning department may be able to help, or even arrange a visit. The children will be fascinated to compare such computer maps, particularly if they cover your own locality. Demonstrate the idea of scale using a simple word processor, by asking the children to type in their own names. Then let them alter the font size so that they can print out their name in different sizes without re-typing the actual names.

A similar activity could be done with a drawing package, using the children's own maps of the classroom and changing the scale using the magnify or zoom facilities in the software. Children will see how a larger-scale map covers less geographical area but takes up more space.

Display ideas

The activity itself will create a display. Supplement the maps by displaying some of the children's photocopiable sheets and some of the 'windows'.

Other aspects of the Geography PoS covered

Geographical skills – 2.

Reference to photocopiable sheet

Photocopiable page 118 consists of two parts. The bottom part is cut off and turned into a 'window' which the children then use to help them gather information from each map, plan or globe. The top part is a table where the children can tick their responses as they interrogate the maps to see whether certain features are present on each.

GLOBES AND WORLD MAPS

To recognise that the globe and world map show the same information but in different ways.

†† *Pairs.*

🕐 *60 minutes or more.*

Previous skills/knowledge needed

Children should be used to cutting and sticking. They will also have to use tracing paper.

Key background information

The way in which we map the world has caused geographers and travellers problems for many centuries. A true model is a near sphere which allows the modeller to depict scaled-down distances as exactly as possible. The land masses and oceans retain their true shape on a globe.

For practical reasons it is often much better to map the world in two dimensions on paper. Transferring the surface of a sphere to a flat surface is virtually impossible without distortion, so many different versions or 'projections' have been devised over the centuries. Two of the best known are the cylindrical Mercator projection, first devised in 1569, in which countries in different latitudes are disproportionate in size and lines of longitude and latitude appear distorted, and the Peters projection, devised in 1973, in which countries at least have their correct relative areas.

The earliest discussions with children about our world and places on it should involve the use of globes and maps. Children are always fascinated by globes and at least one globe should be freely available to them in the classroom at all times.

This activity aims to direct children to some of the basic information contained in globes and world maps.

Preparation

You will need at least one globe and at least one world map for this activity. A solid plastic globe must be used rather than an inflatable one. It is preferable, although not essential, that the world map be of approximately the same scale as the globe so that continents on the map are about the same size as on the globe.

It is a good idea to create a 'mapwork area'. This can be done within a rôle-play area, such as a travel agent's office. There should be enough space for two children to have good access to a globe and to lay out the large piece of paper on which they are making their map.

If you wish to follow the suggestion using green paint as part of the activity you will also need to prepare a painting area.

Make copies of photocopiable page 119 if you are going to use it in extension work.

Resources needed

At least one plastic globe, a large piece of paper (possibly blue sugar paper) for each pair big enough to make a world map at 1:1 scale from the globe, sheets of tracing paper, soft pencils, PVA adhesive, a world map.

You may also need small amounts of Blu-Tack or a similar temporary adhesive, green paint, copies of photocopiable page 119.

What to do

Introduce the children to the globe and the map and explain that you want each pair, in turn, to make a flat world map from the globe.

If the children need proof that it is difficult to turn the surface of a sphere into a flat map, ask one of them to peel an orange in one piece and to lay it out completely flat.

Show the children that one member of each pair will need to hold a piece of tracing paper over each of the land masses on the globe in turn while the other traces around the edges. They should then cut out the traced version of each land mass and, using the world map for reference, stick each on to the large, blank piece of paper to make a world map.

This activity can be made more colourful if the children paint each tracing paper land mass green before they stick it on to a blue sugar paper backing sheet. This will create a traditional world map with the sea blue and the land green.

Talk with the children about the names of the big land masses. Use terms like 'continent' and 'country' but make sure first that the children have sorted out the basic difference between land and sea. The children can then label features such as the Atlantic and Pacific oceans, some of the continents and the UK. If they have used paint it may be easier to add labels, rather than writing straight on to the map.

Suggestion(s) for extension

The problem that the more able children will quickly come across is that some of the land masses, particularly Antarctica, will look quite different, when traced from the globe, from the version on the world map. These children can be set the problem of 'just how do we put these on to the flat map?'.

If the published world map is based on a Mercator or similar projection, the children might notice that the northern and southern land masses, Greenland for example, are smaller on the map that they have made. They will be very pleased to find that their Greenland is, in fact, in true proportion.

Children could name a wider range of places, perhaps using a list provided by you, referring to the globe to find out where they are and then copying them on to their maps.

One fascinating extension exercise is to ask the children to produce a flat map centred on the north or south poles.

Written work on explorers can be successfully tied in with world mapping work.

Suggestion(s) for support

An excellent way of simplifying this exercise, as well as turning it into a group activity, is to ask each pair to trace and cut out just one land mass. If the seven continents are used and each pair cuts out a different continent, fourteen children can work together to make one world map. So with some adult support in the classroom, a class of twenty-eight children can produce two world maps. (One could be UK-centred and one centred on a pole!)

If the children have problems holding the tracing paper in the correct place on the curved globe try fixing it in place with a little Blu-Tack.

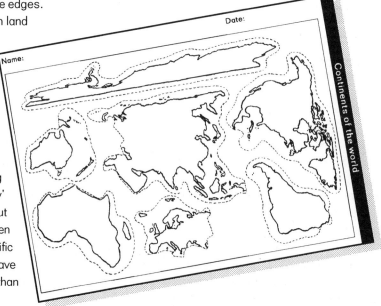

Name:

Date:

Continents of the world

Display ideas

The completed world maps can make a very impressive display. This becomes particularly informative and interesting if the children have created maps which are other than Euro-centred. It may be possible to display a range of published world maps with the children's. Organisations like national embassies and airlines are often happy to supply information which may include unusual world map projections.

If the children have produced writing about explorers, this could be displayed with the maps and don't forget the globe!

Other aspects of the Geography PoS covered

1c.

Geographical skills – 3d.

Places – 4.

Reference to photocopiable sheet

Photocopiable page 119 can be used to reinforce children's understanding of the world map and how it relates to the globe. The continents can be coloured in and cut out then, using either a world map or (preferably) a globe as reference, stuck in the correct relative places on a piece of blank (possibly blue) paper.

Some children may have difficulty sorting the cut-out continents and placing them correctly using the world map as reference. Photocopiable page 119 can be used to help such children get used to placing the continents in their correct relative places.

Assessment opportunities

Photocopiable page 119 can be used to ascertain whether a child can place the continents correctly using a globe as reference. Provide a globe, a copy of the photocopiable sheet and a blank piece of paper (preferably a little larger than A4). Ask the child to cut out the continents from the photocopiable sheet, then stick them in the correct places using only the globe as reference.

Opportunities for IT

Younger children could be shown how to use the circle drawing tool on an art package. The children can also be shown how to fill their circle with areas of blue and add green or brown areas for the land using a painting tool. Children can also do this with a drawing package but they will need to draw the land masses with a freehand drawing tool, making sure that they have drawn closed shapes so that they can be filled without the colours 'leaking' out into the rest of the picture. This simple, but fun, activity reinforces the shape of the world and the difference between land mass and sea.

Alternatively children could use clip art collections of maps and add labels to the different continents, countries or seas using the text commands in a drawing package.

THE UNITED KINGDOM

To ensure that children know that the UK is made up of four constituent countries which, with the Republic of Ireland, make the British Isles.

†† *Small group.*

🕐 *60 minutes or more.*

Previous skills/knowledge needed

Experience in model making, particularly simple papier mâché work, will aid the children with this activity.

Key background information

Children must begin to become aware that they live in a country which is discrete from other countries and is itself divided into smaller units. Young children will need help in learning differences such as those between countries and towns. It is worth pointing out to children that most countries are bordered by other countries and that some have no coastlines at all.

The British Isles is made up of two large islands, Great Britain and Ireland, as well as many smaller islands. The United Kingdom consists of the countries of England, Scotland and Wales and the province of Northern Ireland. The Irish Republic is a separate country and the Isle of Man is a British dependency, not part of the UK.

At this stage children should be aware of the existence and location of England, Wales, Scotland and Northern Ireland, as well as the Irish Republic.

47

GEOGRAPHY KS1

colour. When the model is completely dry, the borders can be drawn on. Discuss with the children whether you need to mark the Irish Republic/Northern Ireland border differently and, if so, why.

Finally, ask the children to make labels with the country names and to place these correctly.

Suggestion(s) for extension

If any individuals are particularly keen you could ask them to make the larger islands of the Hebrides, the Isle of Man, the Isle of Wight, the Channel Islands or even the Orkney and Shetland Isles.

Children could mark the capital cities of each country as well as the city nearest to where they live. They could do this individually on copies of photocopiable page 120.

Suggestion(s) for support

All children should be able to tackle this activity if they are grouped sensibly, but if a child fails to grasp the key idea photocopiable page 121 could be used. Ask the child to cut out the five countries on the sheet and then to reassemble them in the correct places, finally gluing them to a backing sheet. Photocopiable page 120 will be useful in supporting any children who are still unsure.

Preparation

Display a reasonably large and simple map of the British Isles and cover an art table with newspaper or protective sheeting. Gather up a supply of old newspapers suitable for papier mâché work, and a reasonable supply of either tissue paper or scrap coloured paper sorted into five basic colours.

Copy out a bold outline of the British Isles on to a large piece of card. (A trick to help you – if you have an overhead projector – is to photocopy an A4 outline map of the British Isles on to acetate, then project this on to large pieces of card, temporarily suspended on the wall. Simply draw over the projected image.) Restrict the outline (initially at least) to the two main islands of the British Isles.

Resources needed

Art table, suitably prepared, papier mâché paste, a large supply of old newspapers and tissue or coloured scrap paper sorted into five colours, a large, simple map of the British Isles, copies of photocopiable pages 120 and 121 for possible extension work.

What to do

Using the card outline as a base, the children should build up the land area of the British Isles using scrunched-up newspaper. They should then apply several layers of papier mâché newspaper to hold everything in place. Suggest they could find out where mountains are and build this ground up correspondingly higher. Different groups of children could work on different countries.

Once each country is completed its final layers should be applied in tissue or scrap paper – each country in a different

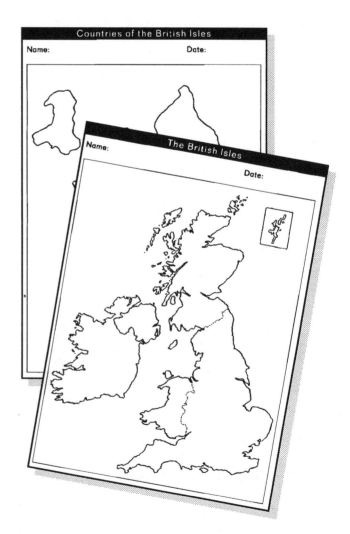

Countries of the British Isles

Name: Date:

Name: The British Isles

Date:

Assessment opportunities

Photocopiable pages 120 and 121 can be used to assess a child's knowledge and understanding of the make up of the British Isles and the United Kingdom. Locating and naming the constituent countries are the most important details.

Opportunities for IT

Children could use a drawing package with a prepared map of the United Kingdom, taken from a clip art collection. They could add their own labels for different countries and major towns. Older or more able children could research and add other names or features to the base map.

Alternatively the teacher could use a clip art file in a drawing package and add a series of labels around the map. If the map and labels are saved on to a disk children can retrieve the file and either drag the labels to the correct place, or use the line drawing tools to link the label to the appropriate place on the map.

Display ideas

The finished model creates a lovely display in itself. Try to position it so that the children can get right around it. A coat of varnish or PVA glue may give the model a longer life and the children will almost certainly want to paint the sea blue.

Other aspects of the Geography PoS covered

Geographical skills – 3e.
Places – 4; 5a, b, c, d.

Reference to photocopiable sheets

Photocopiable page 120 is a map of the British Isles, blank except for the borders. This can be a useful tool to reinforce the activity. Ask the children to colour each country with a different colour and label it with its name and any other relevant details.

Photocopiable page 121 can be useful in supporting any children who need extra reinforcement work on recognising which country is which and where each one is. The countries can be coloured and labelled, then cut out and stuck to a backing sheet (light blue is effective as it looks like the sea).

WHERE DO YOU LIVE?

To enable children to mark where they live on maps of their country and area.

†† *Individuals.*

🕒 *20–30 minutes.*

⚠ *Children may be inserting map pins and, if so, should be warned to behave responsibly.*

Previous skills/knowledge needed

Children will need a simple introduction to plans and maps before they do this activity and will certainly benefit if they have done a little work on their own area and are familiar with a map of the British Isles.

Key background information

It is very important that children, even at a very young age, can locate where they live on a map. In the first place it gives them a point of reference on that map and makes it more 'real'; secondly, it shows that they are capable of actual interaction with a map.

The British Isles map is of particular relevance to most young children. If they can locate approximately where they live on this map it shows that they are beginning to appreciate the geography of their country and its scale.

Maps of different scales should be compared and the exercise of saying 'this is my house; this is where it is in my local area; this is where my local area is in my country' is always most worthwhile.

Preparation

Prepare a large-scale map of the pupil catchment area – this may be available from Ordnance Survey suppliers or the local planning department. It may even be possible to buy a commercially produced one (such as A–Z).

Fasten the map to the wall at a height where the children can reach it and insert map pins.

Display a map of the British Isles to one side of the large-scale map. Prepare lengths of wool or string and small cards for the children to write their names on.

Resources needed

A supply of drawing paper, a large-scale map which includes the pupil catchment area, a map of the British Isles, some map pins (or alternatives if you do not wish to hole the map), lengths of wool or string, some small cards.

What to do

Ask each child to draw their own home on a piece of drawing paper. These should be kept fairly small.

As each drawing is completed it should be displayed on the wall on the other side of the local map to the British Isles map. Each child then sticks a pin in the large-scale map to mark the position of their home. Discuss with the class where your area is on the British Isles map, then add a pin in the right place on that map.

Once the children have fixed their pictures and pins to the wall, they should be helped to run a thread from each picture to the pin marking it on the large-scale map, and then on to the pin marking your area on the British Isles map. Once the whole group has done this all the threads will end up converging on the pin in the British Isles map, emphasising the relatively small size of your neighbourhood on a national scale.

To incorporate an extra level of mapping it would be possible to include a regional map containing your locality; so for London this might be the whole of the south east of England, while for Glasgow it might include the central belt of Scotland. Draw a box on the British Isles map representing the area covered by the regional map. String or wool could then lead from two corners of the regional map to the corresponding corners of the box on the map of the British Isles.

Provide another map so that children born in other places can mark these locations. Other maps could also show holidays or grandparents – even football teams.

Suggestion(s) for extension

Provide more able children with a range of maps which cover your locality and challenge them to find where their home area is.

Children could use similar mapping skills to find other localities studied in Britain. Linking different scales of map based on another studied locality can be a very worthwhile exercise.

Suggestion(s) for support

Children who have problems with switching from one scale to another can often be helped by using aerial and satellite photographs, particularly when these photographs clearly show detail of the area concerned.

It is worth telling the children how long it would take to travel between two places on a map to give them an idea of the distances involved.

Photocopiable page 122 can be used to help reinforce this activity.

Assessment opportunities

Use a blank map of the British Isles and ask the children to mark where they think they live. Initial each dot (if there are several close attempts it might be better to have a different map for each group to distinguish each child's mark). This makes a good game and provides evidence of the children who have a reasonable idea of where their home is within the British Isles.

Opportunities for IT

Children could use an art or drawing package to draw a picture of their own house. They could print it out full size or scale the picture to a smaller size for the display.

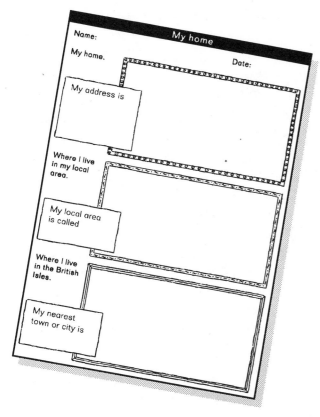

Each child could also add his or her name and address to the picture, or the picture could be imported into a word-processing package where the name and address can be added.

It is a simple matter to re-size the picture once it is in the word processor and to work with the children to make an interesting display of the text and picture together.

Display ideas
This activity generates its own display. In addition a box on each map, linked to the external limits of the previous map, reinforces the way that one map is contained in the next of a smaller scale.

Other aspects of the Geography PoS covered
Places – 4.

Reference to photocopiable sheet
Photocopiable page 122 can be used to consolidate knowledge gained in this activity. Children draw their own home in one box, link it to the location of their home within their local area in the next box and then locate and name where they live on the map of the British Isles in the last box.

Provide a simple line map of the local area for the children to copy into their central box. This can be done most effectively by photocopying the relevant section of a local map on to acetate and then projecting the map on to a white board or screen for the children to copy.

WHICH WAY?

To provide an opportunity for children to make a map or plan of their own classroom and use it to identify simple routes.

†† *Individuals or pairs.*

🕐 *30 minutes.*

Previous skills/knowledge needed
Children should have some knowledge of what a map or plan is. They will also need to know what a plan view is and how to draw a simple plan.

Key background information
One of the first ways that young children use maps is to show the route people take to get from one place to another. Young children often enjoy drawing simple lines on maps to show 'where to go'.

This activity uses the 'end product' of drawing a routeway as a reason for first drawing a map. Once the children have finished the map and drawn their routes they can compare with friends to see if they have come up with different routes between the same start and finish points.

Preparation
Provide the children with paper on which to draw their maps or copies of photocopiable page 123. Make sure they will be able to walk freely around the classroom. Coloured crayons and rulers should also be available.

Resources needed
Paper or copies of photocopiable page 123, pencils, crayons and rulers.

What to do
Talk to the children about how they might draw a map of the classroom. They may already have had some experience of drawing plan views of small objects seen from above.

The children may well suggest that the starting point is to agree the overall shape of the floor, then draw that within the space available. Talk to the children about relative sizes.

It is worth drawing the floor plan on the board for them to copy and, if most of the tables in the room are of a similar size and shape, showing the children how big one of the tables would look on the plan.

Try then to agree what is in the centre of the classroom and what is in each corner. Once these are drawn in the children will find it easier to place the rest of the room's contents.

Let the children draw their own plans of the classroom, then give them a list of places within the classroom that they must visit on a circular route.

It makes the activity more fun if the children are put in pairs and told that they must include their own table, desk or

'place' in the classroom as well as their partner's. Ask the children to draw the circular route on their plan. Once both children in a pair have finished, get them to compare their plans to see if they have come up with the same routes.

Children will soon realise that there are various ways of getting from one place to another. Every time they get to an island of tables or a free-standing display they will have to decide which way to go around it. You could write each stage of the route up on the board and assign it a colour. Instructions on the board might look something like this:

your place	to	computer	blue
computer	to	reading corner	red
reading corner	to	art corner	yellow
art corner	to	partner's place	purple
partner's place	to	hamster cage	orange
hamster cage	to	your place	green

If you are using the format on photocopiable page 123, this will involve the children in filling in a simple key.

Alternatively, children could be left to choose the colours themselves and to fill in the key accordingly.

Each child should then attempt to follow the partner's route. Maps can also be swapped between children from different pairs to see if they can follow each other's routes.

Suggestion(s) for extension

The photocopiable sheet invites children to show which section of their circular route is the longest. An extension activity and alternative to the second half of the activity would be to ask more able children to draw a series of routes to locations in the classroom starting from their own place. This might end up looking like the spokes of a wheel radiating from one location. Children could then measure and/or order the distances to each place.

Suggestion(s) for support

Children will be particularly enthusiastic if the activity forms part of a story. The journey that you ask them to draw could

be the route of an escaped hamster trying to find its cage again or it could be the route of a miniature character from a story.

If you want to concentrate on the route making and not the initial process of the children making their maps, draw a map of the classroom and provide children with photocopies.

Each partner could design a route independently but then go over it in coloured pencil, working together for support.

Assessment opportunities

Keep completed copies of photocopiable page 123. Keep a record of children who have successfully followed other

children's routes. If you provide a recording sheet for the children they might enjoy coming up and writing down the names of children who have completed their route.

Opportunities for IT

Children could record their routes using a word processor so that they can present them for a class display.

A programmable floor robot, such as a ROAMER or PIPP could be used with children working in pairs to program the robot to go around a particular route. If the hall is available this allows the children more space and different objects of furniture can be put out to provide obstacles, otherwise a corner of the classroom could be used, possibly with a large-scale floor plan of the classroom on the floor.

The children could record the instructions that they give to the robot so that another child can program the robot to follow the same route.

Display ideas

The completed worksheets or maps can be displayed very effectively with short pieces of writing by the children describing their routes, particularly if the idea of using a story as the basis for the work has been used.

For an interactive display produce workcards with the children's routes so that pupils can go to the display, pick up a card and follow the selected route. Design cards of your own with routes which take the follower to an unspecified place. Then challenge the children to find what is at the end of the trail.

Other aspects of the Geography PoS covered

Geographical skills – 3c, d.

Reference to photocopiable sheet

Photocopiable page 123 has a large space in which the children should draw a simple plan of their classroom. They then draw coloured lines for the sections of route described at the bottom of the sheet and fill in the key accordingly. They are also asked to identify the longest section of their route.

 FOLLOWING A ROUTE

To follow a route from a simple map.
†† *Pairs.*
⏱ *10 minutes for map making; 15 minutes for playground or hall activity.*

Previous skills/knowledge needed

Children should have had some experience of working in pairs away from the teacher. Some introductory work on maps will also be of benefit.

Key background information

Children must be given opportunities to follow routes from simple maps as this is one of the key reasons for using maps. In adult life we use maps such as town plans and road atlases to help us find our way about unfamiliar areas.

These skills are introduced in this activity, which teaches children how to relate two-dimensional information, prepared by someone else, to the real world.

Preparation

Make a simple A4 sized map of your school playground or hall. Mark a number of 'landmarks' in positions where you will be able to set real 'landmarks' on the ground (see Resources, below). The children will use these to navigate their way around the playground or hall. Photocopy one map for each child and collect together the 'landmark' items referred to above. The number of items you use will depend on how complicated you wish the route making and following to be (between 9 and 15 generally works well).

Resources needed

Between 9 and 15 'landmark' items such as PE cones or stands, beanbags, hoops or chairs, one copy of the plan of the playground or hall showing the layout of 'landmarks' for each child, pencils.

What to do

Set out the 'landmarks' in the school playground or hall as shown on the map. Make sure these are set out in an interesting pattern so that the children will find it easy to relate their plans to the markers on the ground.

Work with one pair at a time. Give each child a copy of the map and ask them each to draw a route from an agreed

starting point to an agreed finishing point. To avoid the children making the route too complex or long it can be a good idea to tell them that their route can never cross itself. Once both children have drawn their routes, they go to the starting point in the playground or hall and have a go at following their own route. If both do this successfully they can then swap plans and try to follow their partner's route.

Suggestion(s) for extension
Children who complete the activity quickly could be given a map of a more detailed and complicated course. This would mean differentiating the activity by planning and creating two versions of the 'landmark' courses.

Suggestion(s) for support
If individuals find the activity too difficult provide them with a simpler version with less 'landmark' items. If a more able child is paired with one less able they could follow the two routes together as a team. This should give the less able child a little more confidence.

Assessment opportunities
It is worth asking the children to report back to their group or class on how well they managed to follow each other's routes. If you have been able to witness the route-following part of the activity then you will have been able to assess the children's ability yourself, otherwise pupil feedback can be useful for assessment.

Opportunities for IT
Children could use a programmable floor robot like a ROAMER or PIPP to practise giving instructions and working out their route.

Provide the children with a simple planning grid and ask them to draw a route which passes through the centre of a number of the squares. It is best to limit the children to about five changes in direction and six moves in a direction. Once the children have completed their route plans they have a go at programming the floor robot so that it follows the exact route drawn on the map. The real skill is in programming the

robot to follow someone else's route.

Children may be able to practise these skills using simple software which is specifically designed for route planning in this way. Children can also use the turtle graphics part of LOGO to program the screen turtle to follow a route or draw a particular pattern on the computer screen. The results can be printed out.

Display ideas
It might be possible to make a display showing the routes that children take when they come to school or of the routes followed for delivering post or milk. Good art and written work can come from books where the story is based on a character following a route, such as:
▲ *Katie Morag Delivers the Mail* by Mairi Hedderwick (Picture Lions);
▲ *The Patchwork Cat* by Nicola Bayley and William Mayne (Picture Puffin);
▲ *Rosie's Walk* by Pat Hutchins (Picture Puffin);
▲ *Postman Pat Takes a Message* by John Cunliffe (Hippo Books).

Other aspects of the Geography PoS covered
Geographical skills – 3c.

Studying your locality

In this section children are encouraged to develop a knowledge and understanding of the world by studying a range of places starting with their own locality. The National Curriculum suggests that places should be studied using geographical skills and that themes should then be studied in the context of these contrasting places. At Key Stage 1 children should be beginning structured study of their own locality. This can provide an excellent context for thematic study and the exercise of geographical skills, including mapwork.

The National Curriculum refers to a school's locality as 'the school buildings and grounds and the surrounding area within easy access'. Once you have defined your locality (the first activity will help with this) you will be able to use it as a discrete geographical area in which to carry out a number of different activities.

Children will be involved in learning about:

▲ recognising their own locality;

▲ the physical and human features and character of their locality;

▲ the effects of the weather on local people and their surroundings;

▲ how local land and buildings are used;

▲ recognising similarities and differences between their locality and others.

Study of the local area will, rightly, lead to children going out of the classroom. It is important to know, and follow your school's policy on taking children out of school.

💻🌳 YOUR LOCALITY

To recognise the school locality as being the immediate vicinity of the school, the area that children know well.

†† *Small groups within the class.*

🕐 *10 minutes for the introduction; 10 minutes for activity in the school locality; 15 minutes for follow up.*

⚠ *Extra adult supervision will be necessary, in line with the school policy for taking children out of school.*

Previous skills/knowledge needed
This activity could be carried out in conjunction with work on 'time' as children will be timing themselves as part of it. Knowing how to use a watch or sand timer to time a period of two minutes will be useful, as will a basic knowledge of maps.

Key background information
The National Curriculum gives a school's locality as 'its immediate vicinity... the school buildings and grounds and the surrounding area within easy access'.

This activity suggests one approach to defining a school's locality. It involves the children in careful use of a large-scale map of the area around the school. Bear in mind that the contrasting localities studied during Key Stage 1 should be of a similar size.

Preparation
Obtain a map of the area surrounding your school; this should be as large a scale as is possible. Prepare an A4 map of the school's surroundings with the school at the centre. At the very least the map should have local roads clearly marked, and preferably named. It may be possible to 'zoom' into the map by using a photocopier with an enlarging facility. You will need a master copy of this map for display and reference and one copy per group. Each group will also need a watch or timer, a clipboard and adequate adult supervision when they leave the school grounds.

Resources needed
One large-scale map of the local area; for each group: clipboard, timer, one copy of photocopiable page 124, A4 copy of the map of the school area, pencils.

What to do
Show the children the very large-scale map of the school's area. Ask if they can locate the school, and perhaps their own homes.

Tell the children that, together, you are going to identify an area around the school where they will be doing some work. Show them how to use a watch or sand timer to time periods of two minutes.

Give each group a route (or routes) from the school so that children will be setting out along a selection of roads and paths radiating from the school. Give each group the appropriate equipment then, under adult supervision, let them follow their given route(s), walking at a steady pace for two minutes. At the end of this time the children stop and, with the help of the supervising adult, mark on the map the place they have got to. The group then returns to class and, once all of the groups have completed their own route(s), a member from each group comes up to the big map in turn and marks the point they got to.

You will end up with a series of dots around the school. When these are joined together you will get a vaguely circular area with the school at the centre. This represents the school's 'two minutes walking distance area' and in future work the class could consider this as the school 'locality'.

It is worth finishing with a class discussion to check if the class are happy with the area that they have ended up with. A housing area may be cut in half, a park where the children play may not be included, or the nearest shops may have been left out. It is quite permissible to alter the bounds of your 'locality' if this seems sensible.

Photocopiable page 124 provides the children with a list of features which they tick to show that they are present in their school's 'locality'. Each group should take one of these photocopiable sheets and tick the features they spot before reaching the 'two minute' point. The class could then combine their findings and fill in one photocopiable sheet to represent the whole locality.

The idea of 'locality' can be reinforced by plotting the homes of everyone in the class on a local map. For most schools the majority of dots will be close to the school, but for those that are further away, ask the children how they travel to school.

This is a very visual way of emphasising the meaning of 'locality' and can bring about some interesting discussion.

The CD-ROM pictures can also be added to children's own writing done on a word processor. In this way the class could write a guided tour of the locality with each pair of children taking a different picture and writing a description of it. The resulting printed pages could be put together to form a book.

Children could also use graphing software to plot the number of children who live in each 'time zone'; either as a bar or pie chart.

Display ideas
Make a larger version of the final map with the 'locality' clearly marked. The locality could be emphasised by enlarging the locality area, cutting it out and backing the vaguely circular shape with coloured paper.

Photographs of some of the features of your local area and pictures drawn by the children of some of these places could accompany the map.

Other aspects of the Geography PoS covered
Geographical skills – 3a, b, e.
Places – 5a.

Reference to photocopiable sheet
Photocopiable page 124 can be used to reinforce the children's understanding of what makes up their locality. The child is asked to consider the geographical area that the class has defined and then tick any features listed on the sheet that exist within the locality.

Suggestion(s) for extension
Some interesting maps can be created if each group marks dots on their route at set intervals, perhaps 30 seconds, one minute and two minutes from the school. These dots can be joined to form a series of circuits. Each sector can be coloured in a different colour, so that the children can then say, for example, 'if you live in the red area you must take between one and two minutes to walk to school'.

It is likely that some children will be more capable than others of this follow-on mapping work. Encourage these children to be the ones who plot the 30 seconds and one minute points to produce the more complex 'zone' maps.

Suggestion(s) for support
Some children will find it difficult to deal with three-dimensional space in this way. Make the finished map as real as possible for them by marking any features and landmarks of particular significance.

Assessment opportunities
As a revision exercise provide the children with a copy of photocopiable page 124 and ask them to identify the features which exist in the locality. Less confident readers may need someone to read the sheet with them.

Opportunities for IT
Children could make a film using a video camera or an album of photographs using a camera to take pictures which show the outer limit of their locality. The film crew could walk round the outer circle, filming landmarks as they go, to produce a circular tour around the school.

If still photographs are taken these could be put on to a Kodak CD-ROM so that children can access them with the computer. They could set up a 'tour' using a slide show facility so that different groups can arrange their own preferred tour.

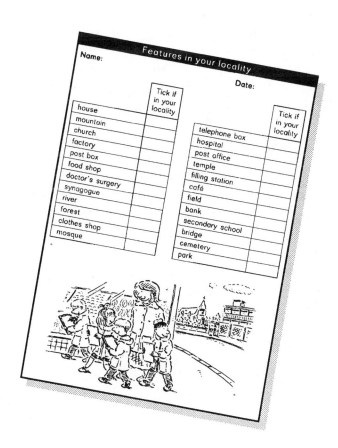

THE PHYSICAL LOCALITY

To recognise the school locality's main physical features.

†† *Individuals within small groups.*

🕐 *15 minutes for the introduction; 30 minutes for a walk or 20 minutes for a brainstorm period; 20 minutes for follow up.*

Previous skills/knowledge needed

Some previous discussion about the extent and area of the school's locality will be helpful. The children should be able to recognise this locality on a large-scale map.

Key background information

Children must begin to recognise that their environment is made up of a vast and varied array of features. Some of these are natural or 'physical' features, others have been created or changed by people and are called 'human' features.

The number of physical features in a school's locality will vary enormously, depending on, for example, whether it has an urban or rural setting.

This activity encourages children to create a 'data bank' of information on the features of their locality, thus focusing the attention of the class on the things that make up their physical environment.

This 'physical environment' can be thought of as the rock beneath the ground, the way that water, wind and ice have shaped the ground into landforms like hills and valleys and the resultant rivers, lakes, soils, flora and fauna.

Preparation

Try doing a brief survey of your area yourself, answering the questions in the following list:
▲ Where is the highest ground?
▲ Where is the lowest ground?
▲ Are there any streams or rivers?
▲ Is there a coastline?
▲ Is there any steep ground, or any cliffs?
▲ Is there any exposed rock?
▲ Is there a place where the soil is exposed?
▲ Are there any ponds or lakes?
▲ Are there any woods or forest areas?
▲ Is there a place with evidence of plants or animals living 'wild'?

Prepare a large-scale map of your school locality and at least one copy of photocopiable page 125 for each group.

Resources needed

Large-scale map of the locality, copies of photocopiable pages 125 and 126, drawing and colouring materials.

What to do

This activity should, ideally, be based on taking the children out of the classroom in small groups to collect the information for themselves. If this is difficult to organise the children can work in a small group in class, 'brainstorming' the information between them from their existing knowledge of the area.

The aim is to find good examples of as many of the items on the photocopiable sheet as possible. The children will then fill in the sheet by drawing their findings.

If they are going to walk around the area themselves it is probably best to decide on the route by considering the questions listed under 'Preparation'. Make sure that you draw the children's attention to the features as you pass them, but encourage them to do their drawing once you have returned to the classroom.

When the children have returned from their walk around the area, or after they have 'brainstormed' their ideas, ask them to draw the features they remember on to the photocopiable sheets.

Once this part of the activity has been completed, let each child choose one of the features and draw a bigger picture of it for display. These pictures can be displayed around the large-scale map with lengths of wool or string connecting each to its locations.

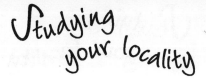

Suggestion(s) for extension

More able children might like to write a description, or draw a picture of what they think their locality would be like if there were no human features at all.

To emphasise the relief of the area (where the hills, slopes, valleys and plains are) children could build a simple papier-mâché model, leaving out houses, roads and other human features.

Suggestion(s) for support

Children could support each other by working in pairs or threes. If they have real problems knowing what to draw, take the school camera and photograph each place or feature. The photographs can then be displayed as an 'idea bank,' for those in need of support. Photocopiable page 126 can be used as a support activity to check that children understand the difference between a physical and a human feature.

Assessment opportunities

The completed copies of photocopiable page 125 will act as a record of whether each child understands which are physical features and which are not. If a child draws a tall building as the 'highest place', then there is an obvious misunderstanding. Photocopiable page 126 can be used as further evidence that children appreciate the differences between physical and human features.

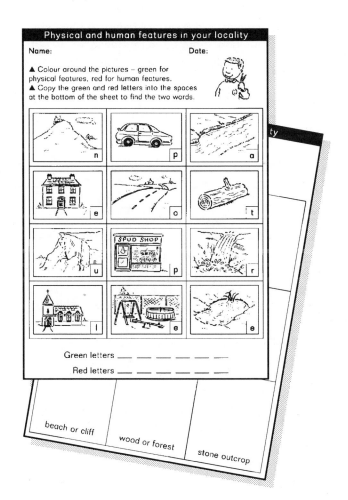

Opportunities for IT

Children could produce an 'image bank' of physical features in their locality using the school camera. These could either be scanned into computer format or the photographs put on to a Kodak CD-ROM so that the images can be used by a word processor or simple desk-top publishing package.

Such pictures could be used within multimedia authoring software so that children could write an interactive presentation of their area. This could include their writing, pictures and even their own voice-overs using a microphone attached to the computer with the relevant software.

Display ideas

The centre of any display should be the three-dimensional model (if you made one) or the large-scale map. Surround it with the children's pictures of the physical features they have discovered and include in the display a selection of their data sheets and drawings. Photographs could also be included in the display. It is most effective to link drawings and photographs of features to their locations on the map.

Other aspects of the Geography PoS covered

Geographical skills – 2; 3a, b, e, f.
Places – 4.

Reference to photocopiable sheets

Children draw the places and physical features listed on photocopiable page 125 to help them recognise their physical environment. This sheet can then serve as a database of information on the school's locality.

Photocopiable page 126 can be used to reinforce the differences between human and physical features. Children colour around the pictures of physical features with green and around the pictures of human features with red. They then transfer a letter from each picture to one of two spaces at the bottom of the sheet to spell out the two words 'nature' and 'people'.

THE HUMAN LOCALITY

To recognise the school locality's main human features.

†† Small groups.

🕐 10 minutes for introduction; 30 minutes for a walk in the local area; 20 minutes for follow up.

⚠ Extra adult help will be needed to supervise children out of school.

Previous skills/knowledge needed

Children should be aware of how to conduct themselves out of school. Simple sorting skills will be useful in this activity.

Key background information

Children should begin to be aware that the features they see around them are either human or physical. Human features are the result of human activity, while physical features are natural phenomena. (Even quite young children will begin to point out that there is very little which is not in some way affected by humankind!) This activity draws children's attention to the wide range of human features surrounding us. Children should start to become aware that many features relate to the world of work, some are connected with communication, yet others are linked to everyday life and leisure activity. They should begin to appreciate the range of materials used in the human world and the ways in which things are constantly changing.

Preparation

This activity relies on organisations' needs to communicate with each other and advertise their presence. Children will be collecting paper and carrier bags with names on, business cards, leaflets, pamphlets and other advertising materials from local businesses and other organisations. Decide on a number of simple routes which will take each group of children past a range of shops, garages, offices, medical surgeries and other local businesses.

Prepare a display area for the materials collected.

Resources needed

A display area in the classroom, extra adult help, a large-scale map of the area for each group, copies of photocopiable page 127 if required to support or consolidate the activity.

What to do

Plan some simple walking routes around suitable parts of your locality. Try to include small parades of shops and offices.

Each group, with an adult, then visits as many places as possible and collects as much 'evidence' as they can. Most receptionists and shopkeepers are only too pleased to provide something with their organisation's name, logo or address on. Failing this, try to get something which reflects the nature of the concern.

Before the groups leave it is a good idea to involve the children in planning which route they will take. Show a large-scale map of the locality and see if the children can identify where they are likely to find different types of human activity.

When each group has returned to the classroom encourage them to sort the evidence they have collected into sets. Some discussion will be needed to decide what the sets will be, and into which set certain pieces of evidence should be put.

When this has been done gather the children around the large-scale map of the locality and ask them if there are any types of human activity for which they have no evidence. Suggestions will typically include parks, playgrounds, roads, gardens and houses (although children may have some evidence of the latter from an estate agency). Ask the children to design advertising posters for these missing features and create some new sets to group these.

Once each piece of evidence has been assigned to a set, display the sets on the wall in a Carroll diagram using strips of sugar paper as boundaries.

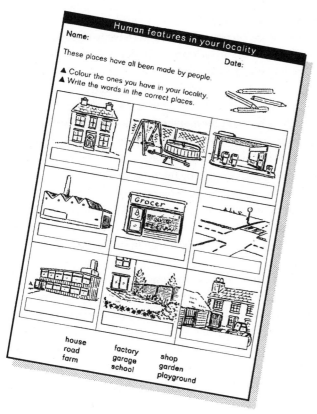

Human features in your locality

Name:

Date:

These places have all been made by people.

▲ Colour the ones you have in your locality.
▲ Write the words in the correct places.

Grocer

house
road
farm

factory
garage
school

shop
garden
playground

Suggestion(s) for extension

Children could use the information that they have gathered to colour a land-use map of the part of their locality that they visited.

Enlarge the map as much as possible and write on the names of all the places from which the children collected evidence at the correct place on the map (if you can get a map which actually has buildings marked, all the better). Back each set of your Carroll diagram with a different colour of paper and ask the children to use these colours as a key for colouring the places on the map.

Suggestion(s) for support

If the children need more support in carrying out the survey keep the groups smaller.

If they seem to find the concept of human features in the environment difficult reinforce their understanding with photocopiable page 127 which asks them to show that they recognise human features which are present in their local area.

Assessment opportunities

During your initial class or group session note any children who seem to be confused by the idea of the human environment. In the concluding discussion ask these children to listen to a list of 'features' and to indicate when human ones are mentioned.

Photocopiable page 127 can be used to provide paper evidence of this understanding.

Opportunities for IT

Each child could use a word processor to write a brief summary of one of the places visited. This could include the name of the place, what it is like, what evidence was brought back and who lives or works there. Children could add pictures to their written accounts, either from scanned photographs or pictures taken from a Kodak CD-ROM. They could experiment with different fonts to make their work more interesting.

Children could display some of the results from their survey using a simple graphing package.

Display ideas

This activity generates its own display in the form of a Carroll diagram. Alternatively the evidence collected could be displayed around the locality map. Word-processed writing could also be included.

Other aspects of the Geography PoS covered

Geographical skills – 2; 3a, b, e, f.
Places – 4.

Reference to photocopiable sheet

Photocopiable page 127 can be used to support this activity. Children identify some human features, name them from a selection of names provided and colour any features which they know are present in their own locality.

OUR SENSE OF PLACE

To recognise that a locality has its own character which is the result of its human and physical features.
†† *Individuals.*
🕐 *30–40 minutes.*

Previous skills/knowledge needed

Some reading and writing skills are necessary for this activity. Children will also benefit from previous discussion of their journeys to school and from work on the physical and human features of their own locality.

Key background information

Geographers talk of a 'sense of place' – what makes a place like it is, what gives it its feeling or its character. It is important that children begin to recognise some of the key building blocks that give their place its character, that make it different to other places.

Characteristics can be very obvious (it's a city, it's a port) or very subtle (you can hear traffic at night; you can smell certain foods cooking).

The activity involves children in identifying some of the characteristics of their own locality and in creating another 'made-up' locality from a bank of possible characteristics.

photocopiable sheet in the box provided. They will come across 'decision boxes' where they have to choose the word which best suits their locality. The outcome will be a short piece of writing which describes the school's locality. The children can then draw and colour a picture of a part of their locality which includes all the characteristics from their piece of writing. If they know that they are going to draw the picture this can actually help the children to focus on the words they will choose for their writing.

Next, the children copy the passage of writing again, this time choosing words which do *not* reflect their local area but a different locality they have imagined. They are effectively making up a description of this place. They can then have great fun drawing what they think this place might look like.

Suggestion(s) for extension
Children who have coped well with this activity could produce creative writing about imagined places and descriptive writing about their own locality. Work on the five senses follows on naturally from this activity. A 'sense trail' around the school's locality can be a very effective way of making children focus on its characteristics.

Suggestion(s) for support
Children who have problems with the reading involved or with the copy writing could be grouped in pairs or small groups with a more able child supporting them. Children are often helped if their finished passage of writing is read back to them before they attempt a picture.

A 'decision box' technique can help children organise their

Preparation
Each child will need two copies of photocopiable page 128 and drawing and colouring materials. Any resources on the local area could be used to introduce the activity.

Resources needed
At least two copies of photocopiable page 128 for each child, drawing and colouring materials, a large-scale map of the local area.

What to do
Talk to the children either as a class or in a group about the local area:
▲ Which bits do you know best?
▲ Which are your favourite or least favourite parts?
▲ What journeys or routes do you often use within the local area?

Talk about other localities (include any contrasting localities that you are studying):
▲ What are the differences and the similarities between your locality and these other localities?
▲ What is it about each of these localities that makes them as they are?
▲ If you live in an urban locality talk about what it must be like to live in a rural one;
▲ if you live inland talk about what it must be like to live near the sea;
▲ if you live in a small community talk about what it must be like to live in a large one.

Each child rewrites the short passage at the top of the

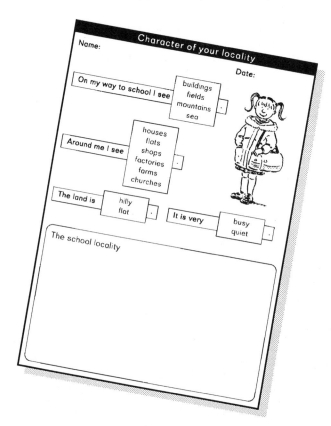

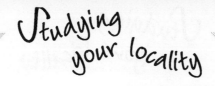

thoughts as they prepare writing. Drawing a picture based on a description generated in this way can provide writing stimulus in itself.

If the copy writing is too demanding, children could simply ring their 'decision box' choices using one colour for their own locality and another for their 'made-up' locality.

Assessment opportunities
If the children perform the task as individuals, photocopiable page 128 will provide some evidence that they are aware of the characteristics of their locality.

It may be possible to annotate the back of the children's photocopiable sheets as they discuss them with you if they provide evidence of understanding about the quality of environments (Thematic Study part of the PoS) as well as evidence relating to the character of their locality.

Opportunities for IT
Children could use a word processor to re-write their descriptive passages. The initial passage could be entered by the teacher and saved as a word-processed file. The children can then retrieve the file, edit and amend the passage, changing each of the descriptive words as they come to them. The amended final passage can then be printed out. If the initial file contains two versions of the initial passage the children can work on the second version and retain the original one for comparative purposes. Children will need to know how to move the cursor around using the cursor keys or mouse, edit and delete words and insert new words and phrases. If the word processor used has a speech facility children can also listen to their new description.

Children could use an art package to draw their new description and add it to the writing.

The activity could also be adapted for younger children using a concept keyboard. The children could read the passage of writing on an overlay keyboard, touching their choice of describing word at each decision point.

Display ideas
An attractive wall display can be generated by grouping the finished photocopiable sheets and pictures. One group could be entitled 'How we see our school locality' and the other 'Imaginary places'. Any creative or descriptive writing could form part of the display.

Other aspects of the Geography PoS covered
Places – 4; 5b.
Thematic study – 6a.

Reference to photocopiable sheet
Photocopiable page 128 is an essential part of the activity. Children copy the passage of writing, choosing the words they wish to use to fill the gaps in order to describe their locality. They then repeat this exercise for an imagined locality.

PRIDE IN YOUR PLACE
To consider the positive physical and human characteristics of your locality.
†† *Individuals.*
🕐 *20 minutes for discussions; 25 minutes for the activity.*

Previous skills/knowledge required
The children will need to have a reasonable grasp of what a flag or banner is. They will also require some drawing and colouring skills.

Key background information
Children must begin to appreciate the physical and human features which give their locality its character. One way of ensuring that children begin to consider the range of features and characteristics which lead to what geographers refer to as a 'sense of place' is to challenge them to design a banner to represent their own area.

Physical features are those which are part of the natural world, while human features are those which have been created or changed by humans.

Preparation
Consider what gives the locality around your school its character. This will be partly a result of the physical world – features such as rivers, slopes, local stone, and partly a result of the human world – with factors such as work places, living places and transport networks playing an important part. Prepare copies of photocopiable page 129, pencils, colouring materials and either a board or a large piece of paper to write down the children's ideas from the brainstorm session.

Resources needed
One copy of photocopiable page 129 for each child, pencils, colouring materials, a board or large piece of paper for noting down words in a brainstorm session. Pictures and photographs which show views of the school's locality will also be helpful.

GEOGRAPHY KS1

What to do

Gather the children together and talk to them about features in the local area which are 'natural' and features which are 'human-made'. Some very worthwhile discussion may be generated, for example, on whether the local park is 'natural' or 'human-made'. The children do not have to leave the discussion with a firm understanding of all the issues involved, but it is important that they are at least beginning to use the correct vocabulary and think about the features that are in their locality. Divide the board or large piece of paper in half and list any features that the children can think of, physical features on one half and human features on the other. Encourage a wide range of features, from large ones such as a factory or a river to smaller ones such as a post box or tree. Write the words clearly as the children will use the lists as a word bank.

Next, talk to the children about flags, emblems, badges, signs, symbols and banners. Share knowledge of well-known examples of these, perhaps the Union Flag.

Tell the children that they are going to design a banner to represent their own locality. Emphasise that this is not just to be a school banner, although the school might figure as one of the human features.

Show the children a copy of photocopiable page 129 and explain that they should choose two features from each of the two brainstorm lists and draw one in each of the four sectors of the banner.

While the children are designing their banners keep emphasising that a good banner is one where all the individual component designs are very simple, clear and bold. Encourage the children to colour their banners to make them as attractive as possible.

When the children have finished their work, gather them together and ask them, one by one, to show their banners. A very worthwhile follow-up activity is to vote on a favourite design and then make a large whole-class banner. The children could make this by painting card and paper, or they could use fabric, such as felt, sewing the parts together or sticking them down with adhesive.

A banner for your local area

Name:

Date:

Suggestion(s) for extension

Some children may want to research their designs from life. If possible allow these children to go and sketch, either within the school grounds looking out or outside the school grounds with an accompanying adult. This would develop the children's fieldwork skills.

Children could go on to design a system for supporting the finished banner (a flag pole, guy ropes and so on).

Children who complete their personal banners quickly could begin to make the larger class banner.

Suggestion(s) for support

Children who find the banner design difficult could be helped by being shown images of features in the local area. Similarly, they might benefit if they are taken out of school to find appropriate features. This might also motivate the children.

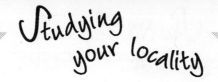

Any children who can't read the brainstormed list should be seated together so that they can be given extra support. They might appreciate a simple drawing next to any words they find difficult to read.

Assessment opportunities

There are obvious technology and art outcomes from this activity, but it is important to remember that the aim is to focus children's attention on learning about the character of the locality. As the children give explanations of their finished banners at the end of the activity, ask each one to talk about why they chose the features that they depicted. Note whether each individual has a genuine understanding of the physical and human features in the school's locality.

Opportunities for IT

This whole activity could be done using the class computer and a drawing package. You could create a template drawing of the banner outline which is saved to a disk. The children can then retrieve the template file, make their own design on the template, save the finished version and print it out.

Children could add their own graphics to the design. These could be taken from a number of sources – they could even use a scanner to make computer versions of their own sketches or photographs.

The completed banner designs could be set up into a slide show using multimedia authoring software and a narrated commentary added by the children.

Display ideas

Ideally the finished banners should be displayed as banners are meant to be displayed – by being carried in a procession. A class procession could form an excellent focus for a school assembly. If the activity has gone particularly well you could even invite local 'dignitaries' to attend! The banners could be suspended from pieces of dowelling.

The banners could be displayed in the classroom by hanging them, in bunting fashion, from a length of string. Alternatively the children could mount their banners on card and cover them with adhesive acetate. Any display should include the words from the brainstorm lists and the images used to generate the finished product.

Other aspects of the Geography PoS covered

Geographical skills – 2; 3a, b, f.
Places – 4.
Thematic study – 6.

Reference to photocopiable sheet

Photocopiable page 129 is a blank banner with four sections. The children could use this to design a banner which reflects the characteristics of their locality. They should be encouraged to draw and colour two physical and two human features in the four sectors.

HERE IS THE WEATHER

To help children understand that the clothes we wear reflect the weather conditions.

†† *Groups within the whole class.*

🕐 *Ongoing activity.*

Previous skills/knowledge needed

Ideally, children should have lived in the locality for at least one year and should have some understanding of the seasons. The activity involves children in classifying and sorting items of clothing and clothing accessories so experience of sorting materials will be useful.

Key background information

Children must begin to recognise that the weather has a significant effect on the way people live. Young children learn this most easily by concentrating on their own clothes – familiar items to which they can relate. They will probably already be aware that weather (and with it their clothes) can change from day to day and from season to season. Children will benefit greatly from learning about the clothes people wear in their own locality because similarities and differences can then be emphasised as they learn about other localities.

Preparation

It may be worth preparing a short letter for the children to take home explaining that you are doing some work on clothing and warning parents that children may be asking for items of clothing to take into class. Prepare some pieces of sugar paper, each large enough for a child to lie on. Clear an area of wall ready to take a fairly large display.

Resources needed

Several large pieces of sugar paper (flesh colour if possible).

What to do

Talk about the seasons with the children. See if they can order them and if they understand that they follow on in continuous rotation. They may know what season Christmas is in, or Easter, or their birthdays.

Discuss what the weather is like in each season. Children will normally start with simple answers, suggesting that it is sunny in summer, cold in winter and so on. Encourage the children to recognise that it can also rain in summer or be sunny in winter.

Once this has been established ask the children how the weather influences the clothes they wear. Allow plenty of time for discussion here as this will emphasise the range of clothing that can be worn in different weathers. Ask what they would wear on a good day in summer and what they would wear on a poor day in summer. Then ask the same about winter.

Put the children into four groups. Ask each group to collect one of the following – clothes worn on:

▲ a good day in summer;

▲ a poor day in summer;

▲ a good day in winter;

▲ a poor day in winter.

Send notes home with the members of each group, specifying carefully what they are responsible for collecting. Emphasise that the items should be the child's own and not adult clothing.

During the period (perhaps a week) that the clothes are coming into school choose either four or eight children to lie down on the large pieces of sugar paper, draw around them and cut out their outlines.

The children can then 'dress' these two-dimensional children (one or two per group, depending on the amount of clothing they collect).

Encourage the children to think about the difference between clothes that could be worn on a good summer's day and a poor winter's day in your locality. The good summer's day outline could wear a swimming costume and the poor winter's day outline could wear Wellingtons.

Once the clothes are all collected dress the cut-outs, then

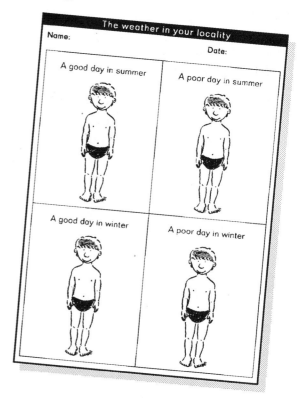

display and label them. The children could make large labels for the individual items of clothing and could also write out labels describing characteristics of the weather for each of the 'people'.

Suggestion(s) for extension

The weather and corresponding clothing words might be used as a word bank for poetry. Children could either write a poem about one of the 'people' or they could write a poem with one verse about each 'person'.

Suggestion(s) for support

If the children find the distinction between 'good winter' and 'poor summer' difficult, limit the activity to just two outlines, one for summer and one for winter. Some children will benefit greatly from this practical activity even if they cannot extend into the written tasks.

Assessment opportunities

Photocopiable page 130 provides an opportunity for the children to demonstrate that they understand how the weather influences people's lives through the clothes they wear. It is best used as a follow-up activity.

Opportunities for IT

The teacher could use a drawing or art package to draw two or four body outlines which are saved as a template file. Children can then retrieve this file and draw the clothes for different seasons of the year on to the body outlines. They will need to be shown how to use the freehand drawing commands and how to add colours.

Display ideas

The dressed figures make a very effective display. Try to make the display as three-dimensional as possible with items of clothing such as footwear sticking out from the wall and items arranged on a table below the wall display. A good alternative is to 'stuff' each set of clothes 'Guy Fawkes' style or even to borrow some mannequins.

Emphasise that the work is on your own locality by asking children to produce a backing display with silhouettes of local buildings. This could be placed behind the 'people' along with a design using rain drops, sunshine, snow and so on.

Other aspects of the Geography PoS covered

Places – 4; 5b.

Reference to photocopiable sheet

Photocopiable page 130 can be used as a follow up to this activity. The children are asked to clothe four outlines of a child according to these headings:

▲ a good day in summer;
▲ a poor day in summer;
▲ a good day in winter;
▲ a poor day in winter.

The children can either colour in the clothes or use collage. They could also draw an appropriate weather background.

THE STORY OF THE WEATHER

To relate the weather to people and their surroundings using a story context.
†† *Individuals.*
🕐 *30 minutes (weather information will need to be noted each day for a week).*

Previous skills/knowledge needed

Children will be recording the weather on a weather chart. They will need to be able to collect very simple information on wind strength, rainfall, temperature and sunshine or cloud cover. This should be done by observation, rather than by measuring the weather.

Key background information

In Key Stage 1 children should become aware of the ways in which weather influences people and their surroundings. From this they should see the importance of recording the weather.

The weather criteria which are easiest to observe from the classroom and by brief visits outside are:

▲ how strong the wind is blowing;
▲ what forms (if any) of precipitation are evident;
▲ how hot or cold it is;
▲ how sunny or cloudy it is.

Wind direction could also be recorded, as could humidity, but it is probably best to concentrate on the first four listed.

Always maintain a simple weather recording chart in your classroom – either a bought one, or one designed by the children or teacher. Ideally this should have space for the morning and afternoon for a whole week and provide symbols for the children to put in place. Only by maintaining such a chart over a period of time do children begin to recognise that there is seasonal variation and pattern in our weather.

Preparation

Make sure that you have a weather chart with evidence of the weather for a whole week. This activity could be done on a Friday afternoon, once the week's weather chart has been completed, or the following Monday or Tuesday, while the information is still fresh.

During the week under study children could fill in their own weather charts using copies of photocopiable page 131. This would then provide them with all the necessary information for the 'story' activity on photocopiable page 132. Take a copy of one, or both, photocopiable sheets for each child and provide a bank of weather words if the children are to follow up their drawings by writing the story out.

Resources needed

Drawing and colouring materials, copies of photocopiable pages 131 and 132 as appropriate.

What to do

Each child requires information on how the weather changed over a five- day period. This may be in symbol or word form – either a class weather chart kept for a week, a child's photocopiable sheet version of this, or both.

Talk to the children about how the weather never stops, but changes frequently. Children's responses when they are asked about whether the weather continues while they are asleep at night are often very entertaining! As a group or class look at the chart of weather information for the previous week and talk about how the weather changed through the week. Encourage the children to share any stories relating to the weather from this period.

67

If the children have filled in their own charts on photocopiable page 131, let them have their own copies of these; and a copy of photocopiable page 132. Explain that they are to make a 'cartoon-strip' style story about the week that they have studied and that each picture should show what the weather was like on that day. The real challenge to the children is that the pictures should provide a real storyline, but every picture should still show clear information about the weather at that point of the story.

When all the children in a group, or the class, have finished their story drawings ask them to take it in turn to show their stories to the rest of the group/class and explain what happens in their story.

The finished stories can be put together to make a class book of weather stories.

Suggestion(s) for extension

An obvious extension to this activity is to ask the children to retell it through writing. The 'cartoon-strip' can provide an excellent stimulus for written story work. Once the pupils have shared their stories with each other (and therefore the stories have been valued) give the children their picture stories back and ask them to write one or more sentences for each picture, possibly on the back of the photocopiable sheet. A bank of weather words would be important here.

More able children could extend their stories to include what happened in the mornings and the afternoons of each day.

Suggestion(s) for support

Children who need a little extra support in their story drawings should be encouraged to consider what makes the progression through the five pictures a story rather than simply a series of unrelated pictures. Suggest that the children do a very simple pencil sketch first and then go back to finish each picture. The bank of

weather words, particularly if they are linked to relevant pictures, will provide immense support to the children while they are writing their stories.

Assessment opportunities

Completed copies of photocopiable page 131 can be kept as evidence that children have been able to relate the previous week's weather. Look too for evidence in the children's picture stories of how the weather influences people's lives and their surroundings. Further evidence might be gathered while the children are sharing their stories.

Opportunities for IT

Children could use a specialist computer application to record the weather on a daily basis. Alternatively they could set up a simple database with each record for a set of readings. The field names might be:

Day	Monday
Time	afternoon
Temperature	hot
Wind	none
Rain	none
Clouds	some

If children work out a set of accepted descriptions for such things as wind or cloud cover and make sure that they only select one of these words the database can be used to search and display graphically for information such as:

▲ the number of afternoons when there was no wind;
▲ the number of mornings that were hot.

Graphing software could also be used to present the weather information.

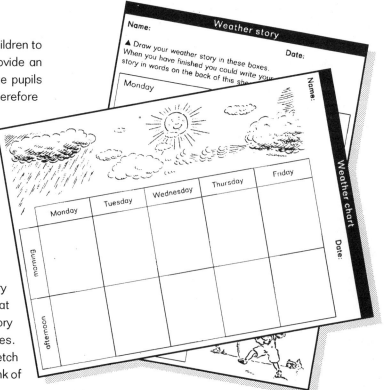

GEOGRAPHY KS1

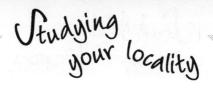

Children could also use a word processor to write their weather stories and decide how they present them to the rest of the class, altering the fonts or sizes.

Display ideas
An effective display could centre around the class weather chart. Display some of the children's weather recording charts (photocopiable page 131) and some of their completed picture stories (photocopiable page 132). The display could be enhanced by weather images and print-outs from the computer.

Other aspects of the Geography PoS covered
Geographical skills – 2; 3b.
Places – 4.

Reference to photocopiable sheets
Photocopiable page 131 provides a simple weather log for a Monday to Friday period. The children can fill this in themselves using simple symbols (they could be designed individually or as a class). Photocopiable page 131 can then be used by the children to support them as they carry out the story activity on photocopiable page 132.

Photocopiable page 132 is a story board with five empty boxes. These should be filled with the children's own illustrations telling a story with reference to the week's weather. This sheet can be used as a stimulus to story writing.

THE WEATHER AROUND YOU

To develop an awareness of how the weather affects local people and their surroundings.
†† *Pairs.*
🕐 *30 minutes.*

Previous skills/knowledge needed
Work on your locality, especially using a large-scale map, will prove a very valuable preparation. Some work on services and facilities in your local area will also prove useful (human features).

Key background information
This activity encourages the children to think about how the weather changes the things their families do with their leisure time. As a part of the activity the children need to be able to consider the range of facilities in their local area.

Children must begin to be aware of the variation in weather conditions in their local area and some of the effects that weather conditions have on people's lifestyles. For example, an area will only have an outdoor facility like a swimming

pool if at least some of the year the weather allows it to be viable. Any area which can have very cold or wet weather is likely to have a range of indoor facilities.

Preparation
Prepare a simple large-scale map of your local area, highlighting any leisure facilities, such as:
▲ park;
▲ children's playground;
▲ sports field;
▲ fishing spots (canal bank, lake and so on);
▲ golf course or pitch and putt;
▲ outdoor swimming pool or paddling pool;
and indoor leisure facilities:
▲ indoor swimming pool;
▲ leisure or sports centre;
▲ cinema;
▲ ten-pin bowling alley;
▲ theatre.

Enlarge or reduce the map to A4-size on the photocopier and make one copy for each child.

Resources needed
A large-scale map with any of the above features highlighted, A4 copies of the relevant part of the map, a supply of red and blue crayons, copies of photocopiable pages 133 and 134 if appropriate.

What to do
Display the large-scale map of your locality with each of the leisure facilities in the area highlighted. Talk about what the map shows and get the children to share their experiences of visiting any of the facilities with their families. This will help any children who don't know what a certain facility is.

Show the children the A4 copies of the map and tell them that they are going to colour all of the places marked on the master map. The places most likely to be visited in summer should be coloured red and the places most likely to be visited in the winter should be coloured blue. Discuss why these colours have been chosen.

Each place can only be given one colour so help the children to see that although a facility may be open all year, indoor places are better suited to the winter months.

If your locality does not have enough features to make the exercise viable it would be possible to expand the range of the map or use photocopiable page 133 which provides a map of a fictitious area.

Suggestion(s) for extension

Photocopiable page 133 can be used to extend the activity if children colour the facilities on the Happytown map red or blue, as before. Photocopiable page 134 can be used to reinforce the idea that the child's locality contains leisure facilities some of which are suitable for summer use, others for winter use.

Children could consider how far their families have to travel to the facilities they use in summer and winter and the problems they encounter with these journeys if the weather is bad.

This activity can also be extended to discuss shopping and the trend towards undercover shopping centres.

Suggestion(s) for support

A much simpler version of this activity is to highlight just two facilities, one for summer, and one for winter. The children colour them with the appropriate colour and mark the routes to them from their own homes. They can then either draw a picture of themselves at each place or write a sentence or two about when and why they go to each facility.

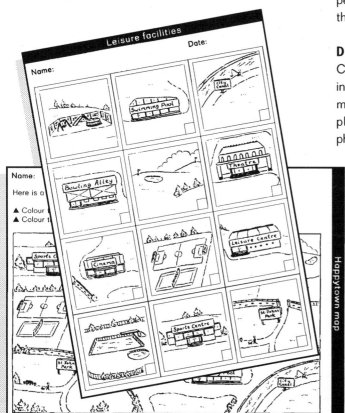

Assessment opportunities

Photocopiable page 133 can provide evidence that a child recognises that the places we visit in our leisure time are suited to different weather conditions and that some are therefore more suited to summer and others to winter.

Opportunities for IT

Children could use a word processor to write about one of the facilities in the area and why they have coloured it blue or red. This writing could be printed out and displayed alongside the map. Children could also add pictures of the facility which have been scanned from photographs, their own drawings or taken from a Kodak CD-ROM.

Children could also use a tape recorder and interview people in the locality about their favourite facility and when they use it.

Display ideas

Children will enjoy making junk models of the leisure facilities in their local area. Provide two table tops, one to display models of places used in summer and one with models of places used in winter. A selection of maps and any photocopiable sheets used could be displayed, with your original large-scale map, on the wall behind the tables. Brochures or leaflets from some of the facilities could also be displayed, as could paintings of the children at each of the facilities.

Other aspects of the Geography PoS covered

Geographical skills – 3e.
Places – 4; 5d.

Reference to photocopiable sheets

Photocopiable page 133 can be used if your local area does not lend itself to the activity.

Photocopiable page 134 has twelve pictures of indoor and outdoor facilities (six of each). The children colour around each picture with either red or blue and then tick the picture if it is of something in your own locality.

PLAYGROUND PLANNING

To partake in a decision-making process as to how a piece of land could be used.

†† *Groups.*

🕐 *20 minutes for the introduction; 25 minutes for field sketching; 20 minutes for classroom work; 20 minutes for class discussion.*

⚠ *Extra adult help may be necessary if children will be leaving the school grounds.*

Previous skills/knowledge needed
Any previous experience the children have had of sketching from real life will be useful.

Key background information
Land is a resource which is often scarce and therefore under demand for different uses. There are many reasons why careful thought needs to be put into how a piece of land is used or changed in its use. Children should begin to appreciate that different people have different opinions on how land is used.

This activity considers the possibility that part of the school grounds could be used as an outdoor play area. To make the exercise less complicated it can be assumed that the decision that the land will be a play area and not something else has already been taken.

The children will consider:
▲ how this designated land could be altered or shaped;
▲ which play activities could be included;
▲ the position of each activity;
▲ the amount of space which each activity will require;
▲ the appearance of the site.

Preparation
Identify an area where, feasibly, a children's play area could be developed. This could be part of the playground or school field, somewhere else in the grounds, or a suitable site near to the school.

Prepare a large-scale map which shows this site and which can be reduced to A4.

Plan the activity so that the children can be taken, either one group at a time or as a whole class, to the site that you have identified. This may involve extra adult support in the classroom.

Resources needed
A large-scale map of the site and an A4 photocopy for each child, pencils, colouring materials, paper and clipboards.

Copies of photocopiable page 135 if required and scissors.

What to do
This activity is best carried out with one group at a time but could be run as a whole class activity. Photocopiable page 135 could be used as an introductory exercise as it introduces the idea of fitting playground activities into the available space.

Gather the children together and talk to them about what makes a good children's playground. Encourage lots of suggestions for different types of activity.

Show the children the map of the site they are going to study. See if they can work out where the site is. Explain that this is the area for which they are to design a children's play area.

Provide each child with a clipboard or a suitable alternative, a piece of sketching paper and a pencil. Take the children out to the site and help them orientate a copy of the map with the actual ground. Ask the children to sketch the area as they would like it to look (preferably with their chosen play equipment in position). This a demanding activity and can be made substantially easier if the children are given assistance in choosing their sketching positions. The adult helper could pace around the site showing them what would be in the background view.

When the sketches are complete, take the children back into class and discuss with them the different play activities they think will fit into the site. Tell each child that they can now choose just five (or whatever number seems most appropriate) activities, and that they are going to have to place them on a real map of the site. Give each of them a copy of the A4 map and tell them to divide the site up into the relevant number of areas and then to map the activities in their chosen locations. They can do this pictorially or by attempting to draw plan views but it will benefit the discussion at the end if the children shade each of the areas a different colour.

Once all of the children have done this get them together in a group and compare the finished maps. Children will have allocated contrasting amounts of land to different activities and this should generate discussion on how they have reached their individual decisions.

Suggestion(s) for extension

Some children might be capable of writing justifications for their choice of activities and descriptions of what their playgrounds would look like. Any particularly keen children could be asked to make models of their playgrounds.

Suggestion(s) for support

If children have particular problems with picturing how the playground would look at the sketching stage it might be possible to use playground chalk to mark possible positions for activities. If children are not capable of the sketching part of the activity provide LEGO blocks to represent playground activities and get the children to place these blocks on one of the maps.

Assessment opportunities

Children could write a brief description of their planned playground, explaining what it would look like and why they have planned it in this way.

Opportunities for IT

Children could use a video or stills camera to take photographs in researching the site. An outline map or plan of the site could be drawn using a drawing package and children could then use the software to design and draw their ideas for the area on to the outline map. They could

also make a computer key to go with the design which would explain the activity in each area.

Children could use a word processor to write about their ideas, perhaps explaining in more detail what each area will be used for and what will be in it. These could be displayed next to the maps.

Display ideas

A small group of children could create a large-scale picture of what a finished version of the playground might look like. This could form a central focus to a display. Picture resources of real playgrounds could be included in the display, along with completed sketches and maps.

Other aspects of the Geography PoS covered

Geographical skills – 3b, d, e.
Places – 4.
Thematic study – 6c.

Reference to photocopiable sheet

Photocopiable page 135 could be used as an introductory activity to give the children an idea of what is required or as follow up. It has a map of an imaginary playground site and five playground activities which can be cut out and positioned on the map. The children have to decide which activity should be positioned where.

Around each of the cut-out activities there is a dotted line. This is the area which has to be left free for the activity to be safe. Children have to make sure than none of the area within the dotted line overlaps with other activities.

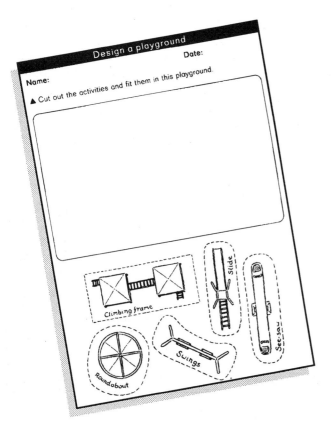

Design a playground

Name: Date:

▲ Cut out the activities and fit them in this playground.

Climbing frame
Slide
Seesaw
Swings
Roundabout

⬙ HOW IS IT USED?

To recognise the many ways in which land and buildings are used in your local area.

†† *Twos or threes within groups.*

🕐 *20 minutes for the introduction; 45 minutes (depending on circumstances) for local fieldwork; 30 minutes for the modelling activity.*

⚠ *Extra adult help may be needed.*

Previous skills/knowledge needed

Children should be used to working in small groups outside the school grounds. They will need to do simple drawings, make box models and use paints.

Key background information

Children should begin to appreciate that land is used in a variety of ways, and that one of the main ones is for building. They must then realise that there are many different sorts of building and that buildings vary in their purpose, shape, materials, size and age. Children will only begin to question why such variation in land and building use exists once they have spent time looking at land and buildings. This exercise helps children to observe and record information about their local area through drawing, model making and painting.

Preparation

Identify a short stretch of road or a part of a pedestrianised area which offers a good range of land and building use and type. This study area should be limited to a continuous line of land and buildings on one side of a road. Allow one unit of land or building for each pair, or three within the group.

Once the units of land and buildings have been chosen, be sure to brief any adult helpers.

Prepare equipment for the children visiting the site and painting materials for their return to the classroom.

Resources needed

Clipboards, drawing paper, pencils, rubbers, pieces of card, boxes suitable for box modelling, paint and painting materials, extra adult help.

What to do

Group the children into pairs or threes and visit the study area. Each little group could either choose, or be told, which unit of land or building to draw.

Explain to the children that as a class they will be drawing all of the units of land and buildings and then making a model of the study area.

Each pair of threesome then makes a simple drawing of their item. If they are drawing buildings tell them to include the number of floors, where the doors and windows are, any signboards and what the roof looks like.

When the children return to the classroom discuss with them how they could go about making a model of the whole study area. The problem of scale should emerge if all of the groups show their drawings in turn.

The simplest way to overcome this problem of scale is to draw parallel lines on the pieces of card that the children will eventually paint on. The gap between each line will represent each floor or storey so this will determine the size of the finished model.

Explain this to the children before asking each group to redraw and then paint their building on to the card. Once this is done it may be a good idea to trim around the edge of each of the building facades.

The children must next choose a box slightly smaller than the facade they have painted and glue the card facade to one side of it. The boxes can then be arranged to form a model street or road.

Children may have chosen units of land such as car parks, builder's yards, gardens, playgrounds or paddocks rather than buildings. If this is the case they will have to draw any boundary fencing or walls and then any features they can see from their vantage point. Their model could be based on a box lid or shallow box. Arrange the finished model along a

table top or on the floor and use it to stimulate discussion. Make sure that the children have learned what each building or piece of land is for.

Suggestion(s) for extension

Children could draw pictures of the finished model and label which building is which.

Children could draw a simple map of the model by looking down on it. This is particularly easy if the model is arranged on the floor. The children's maps could then be compared with a large-scale map of the area. The model can become a play resource if children bring in suitable toy cars; it could then become the basis for work on transport and jobs in the local area.

Suggestion(s) for support

If the children are going to find drawing the buildings difficult prepare an outline which they can work from. Alternatively print photographs of each building or unit of land and let the children work from these.

It may prove easier not to make the three-dimensional model but to display the finished facades in a line on the wall to make a very effective wall display.

Assessment opportunities

Talk to the children about the area they have studied. Can they tell you what each building or piece of land is for, who works there, and about any special features? Ask the children to tell you about the land or building that they drew and note whether they understand its usage on the back of each drawing. Photocopiable page 136 can be used to assess that children have an understanding of the ways in which land and buildings can be used. The children choose two buildings in their local area and draw each in one of the boxes. They then write who lives or works there and what happens there.

Opportunities for IT

Children could take a photograph of each building they are drawing and the class could use these to make a panoramic view of the group of buildings by fastening them together in a line. It might also be possible to scan the photographs into the computer and make the panorama in this way; printing out the final copy with a colour printer.

Children could also use a simple computer database and collect information about each of the different buildings they have surveyed. Keep this fairly simple so that just a few important features are recorded. These might include:

Number	42
Use	house/shop/garage etc.
Storeys	2
Type	detached, semi-detached etc.
Windows	4
Roof	slate/tile etc.

Children could then use the database to search for different information, such as:
▲ How many shops are there in the street?
▲ Which buildings have a slate roof?
▲ How many buildings are detached?

The results can be printed out and displayed graphically using bar or pie charts.

Display ideas

This activity will produce either a large three-dimensional model which can be displayed on the floor or on a work surface, or a two-dimensional painted wall display. The children will enjoy making a roadway in front of the model or

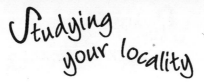

display. Children could produce a 1:1 scale plan of the model by drawing around the buildings on to a large sheet of paper. This could be displayed on the wall behind where the model is displayed.

Photographs, photographic panoramas, the children's original drawings and any completed copies of photocopiable page 136 could also be displayed.

Other aspects of the Geography PoS covered
Geographical skills – 2; 3a, b, d, e.
Places – 4; 5a.

Reference to photocopiable sheets
Photocopiable page 136 can be used to reinforce the idea that land and buildings have different uses and characteristics. Children draw two buildings from their local study area and then write in each one who lives or works there and what it is for.

YOUR PLACE AND OTHER PLACES

To recognise that other places will have some things the same and some things different from your locality.
†† *Groups of four.*
🕐 *30 minutes.*

Previous skills/knowledge needed
This activity involves simple photograph interpretation and so any previous experience at this will benefit the children. Simple cutting and sticking skills are required and the ability to understand a very simple table or matrix.

Key background information
As children learn about different places they should recognise that other places may often seem very different to where they live but that there will also be similarities. This is an important concept in children's learning about the world. As they grow older it will help them recognise and question generalisations and stereotypes. It will also aid the development of an ability to empathise with and to understand people in other places. Learning about the things that are similar can often be a way into a real and balanced understanding of what differs between people and places.

Preparation
Collect together a number of magazine photographs of the same locality, or groups of photographs with each group featuring a different locality. If the children are studying a contrasting locality it would be best if all of the photographs are of that locality but in this case a minimum of one picture for each child (32 images for a class of 32) will be required.

If the class is divided into four groups of eight, each group could do a different locality, thus requiring eight photographs of four different localities. It is important that every image is a different one. This sounds daunting but need not be so if the locality or localities selected are frequently featured in magazines or travel brochures.

Resources needed
A collection of magazine and brochure photographs, a sheet of A3 paper (or larger) for each group, large sheets of coloured backing paper, adhesive.

What to do
Talk with the children about how a place can have some characteristics the same as where you live and other characteristics different. A village in rural India may have a school just like a school in rural Britain, the pupil numbers may be the same and so might most of the subjects taught, but the building and school day may be very different.

Talk about the locality or localities that you have chosen for the activity.

Each group of four children folds their piece of paper into four, opens it out again and then sticks it on to a piece of the coloured backing paper. There must be several centimetres of overlap, particularly at the top and left side. The group then copies out labels to stick above the two columns, one saying 'same' and one saying 'different' and to the left of the two rows, one saying 'buildings' and one saying 'people'.

Out of the photographs available to them the children then have to choose four photographs that will satisfy the labels of the matrix:

▲ one showing buildings similar to home;
▲ one showing buildings different from home;
▲ one showing people similar to home;
▲ one showing people different from home.

The children are comparing the place in the photographs with their own locality. When they are sure that the photograph 'fits' both the labels relevant to it they glue it in the correct place.

If the photographs do not lend themselves to the categories of 'buildings' and 'people' then allow the children to choose others such as 'food', 'weather' or 'transport'.

Suggestion(s) for extension

The children should be encouraged to choose the categories if they are capable of doing this.

If the children are in the middle of studying a contrasting locality in some detail they might even be asked to draw the pictures themselves, thus eliminating the need to provide a bank of pictures for them to glue.

Suggestion(s) for support

If the idea of choosing images to match the labels of the matrix is too difficult limit the categories to just one so that the children are only looking for two photographs.

Mixing the groups so that two more able children accompany two less able will help all of the children to take part in the activity.

Photocopiable page 137 can be used as a follow up to this activity and as such can provide evidence that each child has understood the work.

Assessment opportunities

Photocopiable page 137 can be used by children individually and provides evidence of whether they can recognise the characteristics of a place which are both similar and different to their own locality.

Opportunities for IT

Children could use a word processor to write the information labels for their various pictures on display in the classroom. They could experiment with different fonts and styles to make the labels interesting and easy to read on the display area.

The children may also be able to use a CD-ROM package with images of your chosen locality, if these have been taken in advance and put on to a Kodak CD-ROM for use with this work. The children could print out the pictures from the CD-ROM and add these to writing done on the word processor.

Display ideas

This activity provides a very visual display. Provide backing paper in a range of bright colours so that the finished matrices, and any other display materials relating to the locality, will display in a colourful way.

Other aspects of the Geography PoS covered

Geographical skills – 3f.
Places – 4.

Reference to photocopiable sheets

Photocopiable page 137 can be used as an alternative to the activity or as reinforcement. The children fill in the left-hand labels, then cut out small pieces of picture that they think satisfy both the matrix labels relevant to it. Alternatively the child can draw pictures in the boxes following discussion work in class.

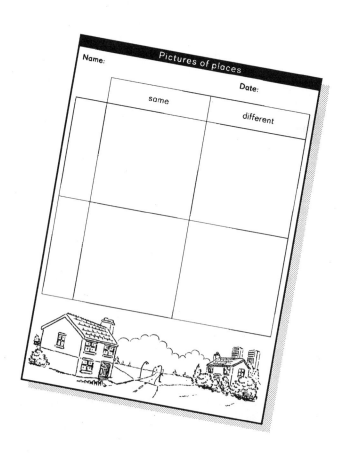

Studying other localities

The previous section dealt with a school's own locality. This section considers how children can learn about other localities.

The National Curriculum recommends the study of at least one contrasting locality at Key Stage 1. This can be either within the UK or overseas. Children will benefit from studying more than one contrasting locality although this will involve finding a range of resources for each locality studied.

It is very important to appreciate that localities studied should all be of approximately the same geographical area as the school's locality. This would usually be an area within easy walking distance of a central point.

Geographical skills and themes should be taught in the context of place study so several of the activities in this section are relevant to certain themes and ask the children to use particular geographical skills.

Children will be learning about:
▲ recognising other localities;
▲ the physical and human features and the character of other localities;
▲ how weather affects people and their surroundings in other localities;
▲ land and building use in other localities;
▲ the ways in which other localities are similar and different to their own locality.

The activities can be used for any locality that the class might study.

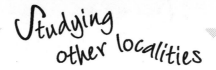

OTHER LOCALITIES

To understand that everyone lives in their own locality, an area which they regard as home.

†† *Individuals/small groups/whole class.*

🕐 *Variable.*

Previous skills/knowledge needed

Children should have spent some time learning about localities which contrast with their own. Simple reading and writing skills are necessary for this activity.

Key background information

Children must begin to study at least one locality which contrasts with their own. Such localities should be of a similar size to their own locality – the school, its grounds and the surrounding area within easy access. Contrasting localities can be in the United Kingdom or overseas.

Children can learn a great deal by helping to develop a resource base on a chosen locality. This activity assumes that such a resource base has been developed so that the children can organise the resources around a map of the locality.

Preparation

Collect together a truly varied bank of resources of the contrasting locality. These resources might include pictures, photographs, booklets, brochures, postcards, tourism feature advertising, maps, items brought back from visits or holidays, items of food from the locality, goods manufactured in the locality, clothing and audio and video tapes.

This type of collection takes time and can provide the children with a very valuable exercise. It may involve the children in letter writing, and the class could even contact a class of children in another school.

Once the bank of resources is assembled, draw a very simple outline map of the locality. Make this as large as possible, preferably large enough to fill a display board.

Resources needed

A collection of resources on the contrasting locality, a simple, large-scale map of the locality, lengths of wool or string and some pieces of paper or card for labelling, copies of photocopiable page 138 if required for follow-up work.

What to do

Let the children help collect the resources. It need not take a long time to make such a collection as a wide range of published resources are now available. Resources can be obtained from:
▲ tourist offices;
▲ travel agents;
▲ embassies and high commissions;
▲ schools in other localities;
▲ libraries;
▲ companies in the chosen locality.

Supermarkets often now label the origin of their foodstuffs.

Display the large-scale, hand-drawn map on a display board in the classroom. Mark on the map the position of any:
▲ schools;
▲ residential areas;
▲ shops;
▲ industry;
▲ leisure facilities;
▲ medical facilities;
▲ tourist features.

Do this in a simple way, don't be tempted to go into great amounts of detail.

GEOGRAPHY KS1

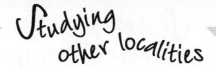

There are two main approaches that children can take to organising the resources. They can either put items on to the display as they are brought in or they can collect all of the resources together and then, with guidance, sort them into groups and decide how and where to display them.

Whichever approach is used, discuss each item with the children and decide how it best relates to the map. An item of food could be linked with string or wool to the shops or, if it is agricultural produce, to the farmland. Try to link pictures and postcards to the places featured. Tourism materials could be linked to the tourist office; goods manufactured in the locality could be linked to the industrial area; any information sent by a school in the locality could be linked to that school. Maps can be displayed nearby as it will be a very worthwhile exercise for the children to interpret them and compare them with your map.

Eventually the map should take a central position with linking threads radiating outwards to the resource items which are either fastened to the wall surrounding the map or positioned on a table in front of it.

Suggestion(s) for extension
Children can use photocopiable page 138 to analyse the locality. It encourages children to carefully 'interrogate' the display.

The activity provides stimulus for artwork based on the display, as well as rôle play, written work and map work. The children could write letters asking for information or materials to addresses included in the resources.

Children should compare this locality with their own and look for similarities and differences. The display could be juxtaposed with a similar one on your own locality.

Suggestion(s) for support
It would also be possible to put the children into small groups or even work them individually, giving each group or individual responsibility for one category of resource. Some children prefer to be structured in this way of working.

Small groups of children could rotate through a support teacher, assistant or parent in class and help to build up the display over a period of time.

Assessment opportunities
Ask each child to select one category from the display, perhaps 'homes' or 'food', and to produce a one minute talk or a piece of writing about it. This would provide evidence of the child's understanding of this contrasting locality.

A completed copy of photocopiable page 138 would provide evidence that the child has understood the concept of interrogating a bank of resources. If children can place the names of resources into the correct columns of this pre-prepared inventory spreadsheet they are demonstrating their understanding of how to sort the resources.

Opportunities for IT
Children could use a word processor to write their own letters to tourist agencies or other providers of resources. They should be taught how to set the letter out and introduced to some simple formatting commands for positioning the address in the correct place, centring their names, and so on, at the end of the lesson. Show the children how to use the justification and centring commands for this rather than using the space bar. The word processor could also be used to design and write labels for the different items in the display.

Children could also set up a simple database showing each of the resources and where it came from. A spreadsheet could also be used for this, to create a matrix where the children enter the information under the correct heading. It might include columns such as:

Number	provided by	picture	artefact	other
1	John	sea front		
2	Balpinder		stick of rock	
3	Rachel			map
4	Mr Jones		model boat	
5	Tourist agency			tourist guide

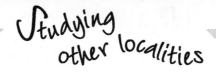

Display ideas

The display which this activity generates will look very effective if it is allowed to 'spill' out on to varying heights of display surface in front of the wall. Do not place the map too high as the children should be able to examine all parts of it in detail.

Other aspects of the Geography PoS covered

Geographical skills – 3d, e, f.
Places – 5a, b, c, d.
Thematic Study – 6.

Reference to photocopiable sheet

Photocopiable page 138 encourages the children to study the display and learn from it. Children draw or write under each of the four titles at the top of the worksheet ('land', 'people', 'weather' and 'buildings') and then write sentences saying what they think it would be like to live in that locality.

PHYSICAL CLUES

To recognise the physical features of a contrasting locality.

†† *Individuals in group or class.*

⏰ *10 minutes for group/class discussion; 15 minutes for worksheet activity; 10 minutes for group/class discussion; 10 minutes for worksheet activity.*

Previous skills/knowledge needed

Some previous discussion of the physical features of your own local area will be valuable here. Children will be saying what they think a locality is like and then, later, have their ideas proved right or wrong, so any work on guessing or hypothesising will be very useful. Children will require simple reading skills.

Key background information

Children should be studying at least one locality which contrasts well with their own. An important part of the children's understanding of this locality will be their knowledge of its physical characteristics, features which are 'natural' and not there as a result of human action. It is worth considering these features when choosing a locality to study.

Preparation

Gather resources about the locality being studied – pictures, posters, travel brochures, photographs and postcards will be particularly useful. Keep these from the children for the first part of the activity. Make copies of photocopiable page 139.

Resources needed

A collection of picture resources about the locality (kept hidden from the children at this stage), a copy of photocopiable page 139 for each child, drawing materials.

What to do

Talk to the children about the contrasting locality you have chosen and tell them to listen hard in case you accidentally give away any clues! Tell them a little about where the locality is and some details on its 'human' features, its buildings, people, work and leisure activities.

Tell the children that they have got to decide what they think the physical or natural features of the locality are like:

▲ Is it high up or down in a valley or on a plain?

▲ Is it by the sea, an island or is it inland?

▲ Is it on steep or flat ground?

▲ Is the ground very dry, are there lots of streams, is there a big river?

▲ Is it very rocky?

▲ Is there lots of vegetation, are there lots of trees?

Provide each child with a copy of photocopiable page 139 and ask them to circle the descriptions which they think suit the locality. Point out that they are unlikely to circle more than one description from each box. The children circle the descriptions which they feel best suit the locality, then draw what they think it looks like based on their chosen descriptions.

Once this part of the activity is complete collect the group or class together and encourage them to share their ideas. Then reveal the picture resources and discuss what the locality is really like. Congratulate any children who have got close to reality.

Display the pictures where the children can see them, then ask them to repeat the activity on the bottom part of the worksheet, this time circling the correct descriptions, then drawing a picture which shows the correct descriptions.

Suggestion(s) for extension

The children could write descriptions of the locality with specific reference to its physical features. The completed worksheets will provide a bank of words and some stimulus for this. The children could then paint larger pictures showing the physical features of the locality – they could even do this at the end of the first part of the activity so that paintings could be displayed in two sets ('what we thought it is like' and 'what it is actually like').

Suggestion(s) for support

Children could also work in pairs, discussing their ideas and supporting each other in decision making. A hesitant child or a poor reader could be paired with a more confident child. If the children seem to be having real trouble deciding which descriptions to ring, gather them together again and talk them through the first one – 'having a go' yourself. Show them some pictures at this stage to give a bit more away.

Assessment opportunities

The completed worksheets will provide evidence that the children understand what the physical environment is. Children will also have demonstrated that they understand the key physical characteristics of the chosen locality. The drawings will provide evidence as to whether the children fully understand what the physical environment is. If they have drawn cars and buses they have missed the point!

Opportunities for IT

Any photographs of the contrasting locality could be put on to a Kodak CD-ROM so that children can browse through the pictures on the computer or use them in their own word processing.

Once the children have made their 'guesses' about the features use a video player and television to show them any available video material illustrating the physical features of the locality. Travel and natural history programmes are often worth recording for this work.

Display ideas

The completed worksheets can be displayed along with any writing or paintings done as extension work. The picture resources used in the second part of the activity could be displayed with the work to make a display which explains the activity, shows what the children have learned and serves as an information source on the locality.

Paintings of the contrasting locality could be displayed alongside paintings showing the physical features of your own locality.

If the area studied contains interesting relief features such as mountainside, coastal cliffs, deep valleys or a winding river, children could make a model using papier-mâché for the land surface. Encourage them to show as many of the features identified on their photocopiable sheets as they can. Display these models in front of wall displays.

Other aspects of the Geography PoS covered

Geographical skills – 3a, f.
Places – 4; 5b.
Thematic Study – 6a.

Reference to photocopiable sheet

Photocopiable page 139 is central to this activity and can provide evidence of understanding. On the upper part of the sheet children ring descriptions of physical features they think are present in the contrasting locality. They then draw a picture of what they think the locality looks like. On the lower part of the sheet the children ring the phrases which actually do describe the locality and draw a picture based on reality.

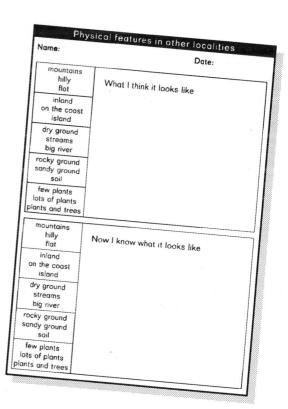

OTHER PEOPLE IN OTHER PLACES

To recognise the human features of a contrasting locality.

†† *Pairs within a group.*

🕐 *5 minutes for the introduction; 25 minutes for the drawing activity.*

Previous skills/knowledge needed

Children should have done some work on the difference between human and physical features. Previous work on using maps and experience of working in rôle will be useful.

Key background information

Human features are those parts of our world which result from human action. Buildings, transport networks, work places and leisure facilities are all part of the human environment. It is important that children can identify these features as being different from the physical environment and that they are aware of the variation in human features from place to place.

This activity asks children to demonstrate their awareness of the human features in a locality which contrasts with their own locality. They do this by pretending that they live in the contrasting locality.

Preparation

Prepare a map of the contrasting locality and some photographs or other images of it.

The children will need some white drawing paper of a reasonable size (A3 is suitable) and drawing and colouring materials. Copies of photocopiable page 140 can be used as an alternative to the large pieces of paper. Identify several places on the map of the contrasting locality which are part of the human environment and which the children will understand. These might include:

▲ a post office;
▲ a shop;
▲ a block of flats;
▲ a house;
▲ a hospital;
▲ a police station;
▲ a harbour;
▲ a railway station.

Mark these locations on the map by fixing small labels which contain a simple symbol or the name of the place.

Resources needed

Large pieces of white drawing paper (possibly A3) or copies of photocopiable page 140, a large-scale map and picture resources of the contrasting locality, small labels, drawing and colouring materials.

What to do

Show the children the map with the small symbols or locality names marked on it. Look at pictures or photographs of the locality and discuss the human features in the pictures. Children are always fascinated by means of transport in other places and in differences in building design or function. Tell each pair of children that they have to choose two of the locations identified on the map and decide on a route between them. They will not be starting at the same point. The route may involve use of footpaths, roads, a railway or even a river or canal. Each child in the pair then decides on a location to start from.

The children then separate and draw what they think their starting locations might look like. They then draw the route across their paper from their location to the location where their partner is starting. Their partner carries out the same activity from the other starting point. On the route between the two locations each child draws any features which the map or their imaginations suggest might be there. Both children then draw their finishing location as they think it might look.

Once everyone has finished it is great fun to bring the children together and to see how similar or different each pair's features and routes are. Look particularly for any details which demonstrate an understanding of the locality.

The children will enjoy drawing themselves as a person who lives or works at their starting location travelling between the two places.

82

Suggestion(s) for extension

Children could produce writing which has both a descriptive and a creative component to it, telling about their journey between the locations. This could be written in the first person or in the third person if the children are capable of 'putting themselves into someone else's shoes'.

In their pairs the children could make up a story about their two characters and the two places.

Suggestion(s) for support

Sketch the line of the route between the two locations chosen by the children to make this part of the activity easier.

The whole activity would be much more straightforward if the number of locations was limited – possibly even to just two locations (although this would obviously limit the amount the children would learn about the locality).

Assessment opportunities

Examine the completed drawings and note if the children have understood what their start and finish features are and if their drawing of these features and other features on the route are appropriate for the locality. Photocopiable page 140 can also be used as evidence.

Opportunities for IT

Children could use a word processor to record the directions for following the route they have marked on the map and note any features that they pass on the way. Tell the children that they are going to send the instructions to someone who is visiting the locality, so they must be certain that they are clear and accurate.

Display ideas

The completed drawings will look very effective displayed around the original map of the locality. Picture resources on the locality could be displayed between the drawings, with any which actually show a feature that a child has drawn linked to it.

Other aspects of the Geography PoS covered

Geographical skills – 2; 3a, d, e, f.
Places – 4; 5d.

Reference to photocopiable sheets

Photocopiable page 140 offers an alternative to using large sheets of paper. It provides the child with spaces to draw their starting and finishing places and then a large space in which they draw the two features again with the route between them.

WHAT'S IT REALLY LIKE?

To be able to question what it is about a locality that gives it its character.

†† *Individuals.*

🕒 *40–60 minutes.*

Previous skills/knowledge needed

Children should have spent some time studying the contrasting locality and have considered its human and physical features. This activity requires simple message-writing and drawing skills.

Key background information

Geographers talk of having a 'sense of place', an understanding of what makes a place feel and look like it does. Many of the places that children learn about are too far away for them to gain any direct experience but it is important to ensure that they gain at least a reasonable understanding of the character of such places.

The children will need to have some knowledge of the locality as this activity is meant to demonstrate that they understand its overall character. They are asked to draw some pictures to make a postcard of the place they are studying. They are also required to write a message saying what the place is like.

Preparation

Collect together any available picture or video resources of the locality so that they can be used to set the scene.

Prepare a number of small pieces of thin card cut in the dimensions of the postcards on photocopiable page 141.

Resources needed

Thin card cut in the dimensions of the postcards on photocopiable page 141, glue, scissors, copies of the photocopiable sheet, drawing and colouring materials.

What to do

Explain to the children that they must choose the five most noteworthy features of the locality that they think would represent it best on a picture postcard. They must then decide what they would say about the place if they were sending a postcard to their parents or somebody else who had never been there. Tell the children that it is important that their postcard gives a comprehensive feeling of the place they have been studying because the people they are sending it to might never be able to go there.

Talk to the children about the different features that they could draw and write about. They could depict human and physical features and places that show both.

It might be helpful as an introductory exercise if, as a group or class, you designed a postcard to send from where you live.

The children then draw their pictures and write their descriptive messages in the relevant places on the postcard formats on their copies of photocopiable page 141. It is a

good idea to hold a 'brainstorming' session, encouraging the children to suggest words which might be used to describe the locality. Copy these words out on the board and use them as discussion stimulus in the early stages.

Once the children have filled in their 'postcards' help them to cut them out and to stick one on each side of a piece of thin card. Try to use a glue that will not warp the paper too much. Children could also design a suitable stamp for the locality and stick one in the relevant place (or simply draw it straight on to the postcard).

Suggestion(s) for extension

Much can be done with real postcards from the locality being studied. These can be sorted and classified, they can be the subject for descriptive writing and they can be stimulus for art work.

The class could go on to produce a tourist brochure about the locality.

Children can also have great fun producing postcards and brochures for their own locality.

Suggestion(s) for support

The activity could easily be restricted to children simply drawing the pictures for the front of the postcard.

If you would like all or most of the children to do some writing as part of the activity, have an introductory session in which the class as a whole identifies ten or twelve simple sentences, each describing something important about the locality. Write these up on the board, then ask each child to choose an appropriate number of these and to write them on to the postcard.

Assessment opportunities

The finished postcards should provide evidence that the children have an understanding of the things that give the locality studied its character. A child with a good

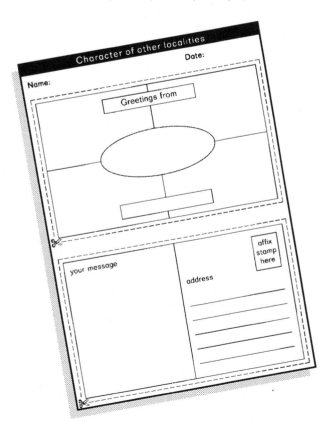

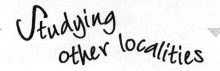

understanding will probably produce a postcard which includes evidence about the weather, the physical features of the area and any human features and activities.

If more evidence is required, children could read their postcards and discuss them with the group. This would provide an opportunity to note down any extra information that they mention.

Opportunities for IT

Children could design their postcards using a word processor or simple desk-top publishing package. The teacher could set up a template for the postcard beforehand with one side for the picture and the other for the writing. Children may be able to add pictures scanned from photographs or taken from CD-ROMs.

Display ideas

If your locality is overseas find out what a letter box would look like. Then cut out and paint a large letter box front which can be fastened to the wall as a backing to the display. The cards themselves should be attached to a 'washing line' of string so that each card can be turned, allowing both sides to be seen. Use picture resources or other pieces of work on the locality to enhance the finished display.

Other aspects of the Geography PoS covered

Geographical skills – 3a, f.
Places – 4; 5b, c, d.

Reference to photocopiable sheet

Photocopiable page 141 provides a format to help children produce a postcard. They must draw and colour images of the locality being studied in one of the panels and write a message in the other.

The two panels are then stuck either side of a piece of card to make the completed postcard.

HOW'S YOUR WEATHER?

To consider how the weather affects a contrasting locality and the people who live there.

†† *Pairs or fours within groups.*

⏱ *15 minutes for discussion; 35 minutes for the activity.*

Previous skills/knowledge needed

Children should do this activity in the context of wider study about a locality which contrasts with their own. Some knowledge of the locality will be useful, as will some understanding about weather. Children should have watched television weather forecasts, and will need drawing and colouring skills.

Key background information

When children are studying a locality which contrasts with their own, the weather is one of the most obvious things that give a place its character.

Children should start to become aware of how the weather in a place affects the place itself and influences the lives of the people who live there.

In this activity children colour weather symbols relevant to the locality being studied, cut them out and then use them to present a simple weather forecast for the locality.

Preparation

Obtain a large-scale map of the area being studied and make copies of photocopiable pages 142 and 143 as appropriate. Check that the children are aware of the types of weather found in the locality they are studying.

Resources needed

A large-scale map of the contrasting locality, copies of photocopiable pages 142 and 143 if required, Blu-Tack, colouring materials.

What to do

Talk with the children about what they wear in different weathers and at different times of year. Discuss how some people are badly affected by the weather such as farmers in a drought or the danger of living near a river during a heavy rainfall.

Move on to discuss these subjects in the context of the locality being studied. A large-scale map of the locality may be helpful as you discuss the weather in the locality and its effects on people and their surroundings.

Ask each child to choose the symbols on photocopiable page 142 which they think will be relevant to the locality. They should then colour and cut them out. Next, challenge each child to present a weather forecast for the locality, using the large-scale map and the symbols (with some Blu-tack to help them stick).

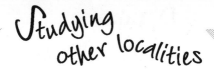

Children could record their understanding of what the weather is like in the locality and how it affects people's lives by filling in a copy of photocopiable page 143. This provides a format for writing down the forecast, and three key questions relating to people and, their surroundings.

Suggestion(s) for extension

The weather forecasts could be prepared by groups of four working co-operatively to prepare not only a forecast for the contrasting locality, but also for their own. This will emphasise the similarities and differences between the two localities. Children should explain what time of year their forecast is for.

Children could produce their own maps of the locality, sticking on coloured-in symbols from photocopiable page 142 to make a weather map. Weather maps made like this can then be linked with completed copies of photocopiable page 143. This will provide a comprehensive explanation of the type of weather typical of the area, the type of clothing most likely to be worn, the kinds of place that people might go in the weather being described and the local people who will need to know about the weather (perhaps fishermen if it is a coastal area).

Suggestion(s) for support

Working in pairs or fours will allow children who are more likely to find this activity difficult to be grouped with others who will support them.

It is important that children make up and write weather forecasts which might be genuine for the locality. Some children may find it helpful if the most suitable words in the word bank on photocopiable page 143 are highlighted for them.

If the children are working in groups of four, one could put the symbols on the map as another passes them, while

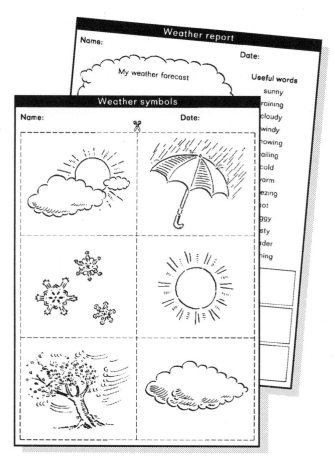

a third reads the forecast. The fourth member could then tell everyone what clothes would be best to wear, which places they would recommend going to as a result of the weather and which local people are most likely to need to know about these weather conditions.

Assessment opportunities

For written evidence of understanding children could complete photocopiable page 143. This will provide evidence that they understand about the effects of weather on people and their surroundings.

Opportunities for IT

Use a television to show the children real television forecasts for their own area. The children could use a video camera to video themselves giving their own forecasts and then play back these 'broadcasts' using a video player and monitor.

A map of the area could be scanned so that it could be used with a computer drawing package. Weather symbols could be drawn by the teacher or the children themselves and these could be positioned in the relevant places on the map. A short written forecast could also be added. Children could also look at local forecasts from the paper and use a word processor to write their own short forecast for the locality.

Display ideas

The large-scale map of the contrasting locality with the symbols from photocopiable page 142 will create an effective

interactive display. This could be enhanced by displaying the children's own weather maps of the locality alongside. If the weather in the locality you are studying varies from season to season weather maps depicting each of the seasons could be displayed.

If the map is displayed at a level easily reached by the children with a supply of the weather symbols coloured in (and even mounted on card) children can enjoy doing their own weather forecasts.

Other aspects of the Geography PoS covered
Geographical skills – 3a, e, f.
Place – 4; 5b.

Reference to photocopiable sheets
Photocopiable page 142 can be used to provide symbols for use by children making up weather forecasts. Each symbol should be coloured in, cut out, and can then be stuck on to card.

The children can use photocopiable page 143 to write their weather forecasts on. A bank of useful words is provided as stimulus. The three questions asked encourage the children to show their understanding of how the weather affects people and their surroundings in the locality being studied.

This activity encourages the skills of resource interpretation and model making to improve the children's knowledge and understanding of the contrasting locality.

Preparation
Prepare a bank of resources on the locality you are studying. Photographs, postcards, posters, brochure pictures and other resources which show what the land and buildings look like will be particularly useful.

A large-scale map of the locality will be needed to help with placing each building on a layout once they are all finished. The plan will also be very useful as part of a final display of the work.

Collect together a range of modelling materials including paper, paint, glue and scissors. Copies of photocopiable page 144 can be used by the children to help them plan their models.

▣ MODEL PLACES

To be aware that land and buildings are used in ways which are characteristic of their locality.

†† *Pairs within a group.*

🕐 *15 minutes for discussion; 35 minutes for model making.*

Previous skills/knowledge needed
Children should do this activity as a part of wider work on a locality which contrasts with their own. Ideally children will already have a good 'feel' for the locality in question and will already have had their attention drawn to the types, styles and functions of the land and buildings there.

Children will need to know how to make a simple junk model and how to use materials such as paint and glue.

Key background information
Children must begin to develop an understanding of how and why land and buildings are used in other localities. Different places have different patterns of land use as a result of such things as terrain, climate and types of economic activity. Building styles will reflect such things as the climate and the materials available.

Young children should realise that the area they are studying will have land and buildings with certain characteristics. They will notice both similarities to and differences from the land and buildings where they live.

Resources needed
A large piece of card, paper or board to act as a base for the model, a collection of junk and boxes suitable for modelling, paint, card, glue, scissors. Copies of photocopiable page 144 if the children will be using them for planning.

What to do
Tell the children that they are going to make a model a bit like a model village. They will work in pairs and each pair will make one building or one area of land (perhaps a farmyard, a playground or a beach area). Explain that they will not be able to make an exact model of the locality you are studying but will be trying to model a good range of the buildings to make as good a representation as possible.

Share out or display the picture resources about the locality so that all of the children involved have access to them. Pair the children and decide which building will be made by each pair. Point out to the children that the end result will be much better if an approximate scale has been agreed. One way of doing this is to provide the children with pieces

more time to examine the resources and plan their models. Photocopiable page 144 will help children to focus in on the building they have chosen.

Providing them with boxes of the correct approximate size will support them in making their model.

Assessment opportunities

This activity offers three opportunities for assessing the children's understanding:

▲ during the discussion and organisation of resources;

▲ by looking at completed copies of photocopiable page 144;

▲ when the children are discussing the completed model.

The first and third will involve some extra note taking.

Opportunities for IT

For UK localities the children could use framework software like *My World 2* and the *Design a 3D House* resource file to help them design and make the models for their locality. Once the house has been designed it can be printed out in a net form, stuck on to card, cut out and glued together.

For other localities children could use picture resources from CD-ROM to provide information on the types and styles of buildings.

Display ideas

The activity will create a very impressive, large table top or floor display. Any plan that is made can be hung on the wall behind the model.

The children can then paint in the roadways, pathways and other surface features of the land. The base board should

of thin card to use for the fronts of their buildings which have parallel lines drawn on as guides for each storey or floor. Another way is to say that a toy construction brick, for example, represents the size of all the doors.

Try to make sure that a range of buildings are chosen. If the children are using the planning sheet they will draw both the front and the rear of the building. This should help them focus in on what the building is really like. The sheet also encourages them to label the parts of the building and note the materials used.

Next the children make their buildings, including as much detail as possible. The buildings can then be arranged on the base board or card to represent the overall appearance of the locality you are studying. Some final details may help to ensure that the model has the correct overall character as your work on the locality progresses. Further details may be added later.

Suggestion(s) for extension

It may be possible to draw around each of the finished buildings to create a plan of the place you have created. This plan can be displayed behind the finished model, reinforcing the idea of the plan view. Children could even use colour coding, symbols and a key on the map.

Photocopiable page 144 could also be used for buildings in your own area to reinforce understanding of how localities have similarities and differences.

Suggestion(s) for support

Pair a less able pupil with a more able one. Children may appreciate a longer period of discussion at the outset and

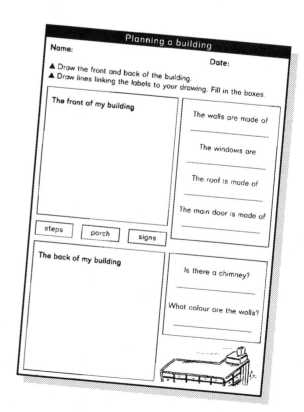

also reflect the character of the land in the locality.

Completed copies of photocopiable page 144, the original picture resources and the large-scale map can also be displayed around the model.

Other aspects of the Geography PoS covered

Geographical skills – 3d, e, f.
Places – 4; 5a, b, c.

Reference to photocopiable sheet

Photocopiable page 144 can be used to help plan this activity or independently. Children draw the front and rear of a building they are studying and label each part, indicating the materials that have been used.

OTHER PLACES – THE SAME BUT DIFFERENT

When children learn about another locality they will notice some similarities and some differences between it and their own.

†† *Individuals.*

🕐 *15 minutes for the introduction; 30 minutes for poem writing.*

Previous skills/knowledge needed

Children should be studying a locality which contrasts with their own local area. This activity encourages the children to compare these localities so some knowledge of the children's own locality is essential.

The activity encourages the children to recognise similarities and differences and then to record them in poetry. It will not matter if the children have not written poems before.

Key background information

It is important that children come to realise that places have their own character, resulting from any number of physical and human features. It is a very worthwhile exercise for children to consider similarities and differences between their own locality and others. Recognising and understanding the similarities can help the children to develop empathy for people who live in other places and can also make understanding the differences easier.

In this activity the children develop their understanding by writing poems. This 'mechanical' approach has a definite structure which gives the child a lot of support.

Preparation

Provide resources on both your own and the contrasting localities being considered. It might be worth noting down some of the obvious similarities and differences before starting discussions with the children. Make two copies of photocopiable page 145 for each child.

Resources needed

Paper, writing, drawing and colouring materials, copies of photocopiable page 145.

What to do

Ask the children what a poem is and discuss this with them. Emphasise that the lines of a poem are not necessarily like sentences but can be groups of punchy words which give a feeling or sum something up. Explain what a verse is and tell the children that they are each going to write two one-verse poems, one about your own locality and one about the contrasting locality. Explain that everyone is going to use the same method to make their poems but that when they have finished all the poems will be different.

Take some time to discuss the two localities – particularly the things which are similar and the things which are different. Try to get the children to concentrate on these in their work.

Give each of the children the copies of photocopiable page 145 and explain that the boxes around the poem space are for them to write down words they may use in that line.

The first line of each verse is simply the name of the locality, but encourage the children to write a number of relevant words in each of the planning boxes. Once they have done this they can choose the best words, rearrange them and copy out the final lines in the poem box.

Suggestion(s) for extension

Children could write their poems on a particular theme such as 'buildings' or 'food' in the localities. They could write longer poems with more verses.

Children might enjoy copying their poems out on to another piece of paper and drawing a border of pictures illustrating the contents of the poem.

Encourage children to attempt rhyming poems which have more of a sentence style of construction.

Suggestion(s) for support

Some children may need a fair amount of support with this activity. The class could brainstorm the words so that the teacher could then copy the words into the planning part of the photocopiable page and photocopy sheets for the children.

Certain children will feel more secure with a reasonable level of adult support so that they can have the words that they think of written out as they think of them.

Some children will produce better poems by working in a truly individual situation rather than in a group of children all working to the same end.

Assessment opportunities

The finished poems provide part evidence of the children's understanding and knowledge of how the two localities compare.

If the activity has gone well it can be a very satisfying experience to hold a poetry reading session (some children could read their own poems, others may prefer adult help). At this stage the children could be asked to clarify their understanding of the similarities and differences between the two localities. The poems will provide evidence relevant to the English curriculum as well as geography.

Opportunities for IT

The children could use a word processor to write their poems, either individually or in pairs. Some children may be able to add pictures taken from scanned photographs or CD-ROMs to illustrate their poems. The final versions can be printed out and displayed in the classroom. Children could also record their own readings of their poems. These recordings could be used with the printed versions in the listening corner of the classroom.

Display ideas

Display the finished poems on the wall with picture resources on the two localities. If the children have copied their poems on to fresh sheets of paper and illustrated the poems around the edge then the display will be further improved.

Other aspects of the Geography PoS covered

Geographical skills – 3a, f.
Places – 4.

Reference to photocopiable sheet

Photocopiable page 145 provides children with a planning and writing sheet to help them write two simple poems illustrating the contrasts between their own and another locality.

Each poem should be on one locality and the first line of each poem will simply be the name of that locality.

Children should look at the suggested content for each line in the planning boxes. They then write as many words as they can think of which are relevant in these boxes.

Finally they decide on the words they will use and their order, and then write the finished line in the poem box. When they have done this for every line they will have a finished poem. When they read it through they may wish to alter it slightly to improve its overall sound.

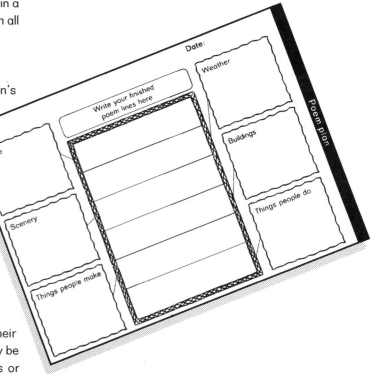

Studying environmental quality

At Key Stage 1 the National Curriculum requires that children make a study of the quality of the environment in a locality, either in the United Kingdom or overseas. This is the only thematic study that Key Stage 1 children are required to carry out, but it is possible to cover part of the geography curriculum through the study of other themes.

This section provides activities which support learning about environmental quality. Choose a locality with great care. Work on your own locality can be very rewarding as the children can get some experience of fieldwork and can get directly involved in the issues. If a distant locality is chosen it is important to have a satisfactory supply of resources.

The nature of the environment can be either human or physical and the study could involve issues which concern both. Activities in this section involve children in:
▲ expressing views on the attractive and unattractive features of an environment;
▲ recognising how an environment can change;
▲ studying how environmental quality can be sustained and improved.

Children should become increasingly aware that the world changes in all sorts of ways and that different people have different views on what they like or don't like and on whether things should be changed or left as they are. Work on this theme should encourage children to develop a caring attitude towards the environment as a whole.

◆ LIKES AND DISLIKES

To learn that environments have attractive and unattractive features and that views on such features differ.

†† *Pairs within a group or class.*

🕐 *10 minutes for the introduction; 20 minutes for activity in school grounds; 15 minutes for classroom activity.*

Previous skills/knowledge needed

Children will need to know the 'bounds' of the school and where they are allowed to go.

The activity requires some simple drawing skills, particularly working outside the classroom using clipboards.

Key background information

Children should be beginning to express clear and reasoned views on what they like and dislike about a place. This forms part of their learning about the quality of environments including the skill of careful observation.

Children should be given opportunities to express views on environmental quality in a range of locations.

Preparation

Prepare copies of photocopiable page 146. Collect drawing and colouring materials and some paper suitable for the children to stick their finished pieces of work on to.

Resources needed

Two copies of photocopiable page 146 for each child, pieces of paper of A4 size or larger (this could be coloured paper), clipboards, a range of pictures of different types of places, glue, colouring materials.

What to do

Gather the children together and discuss the collection of pictures of different places. Make this collection of images as varied as possible, some of the countryside, some of urban areas. Ask the children to point out places they prefer and others they don't like. Ask them to explain their preferences and encourage some disagreement between the children. Use the disagreements to emphasise that we all have different views about what we like to look at.

Put the children into pairs and ask each pair to walk around the school grounds. Each child takes a clipboard and two copies of photocopiable page 146 and together they decide on four places within the school grounds which they can draw. Tell them to choose four places which are as different as possible and that each child in a pair should draw the same views.

As the children return give them some time to improve their drawings and colour them in, then ask each person in the pair to sit separately.

Each child should now complete the two sentences under the four pictures. These sentences start, 'Things I like about this place are... ' and 'Things I dislike about this place are....'

Provide each child with a piece of backing paper, a pair of scissors and some glue. Explain that once they have completed their writing they must cut out each of the pictures (with the sentences attached) and put them in order with their favourite place first and least favourite last. Once this is done the children stick the four cut-outs, in order, on to the backing paper.

Ask each pair to get back together and to see if they have chosen the same order for their places. Finish with a group or class discussion about the variation in people's choices.

Suggestion(s) for extension

This activity can be used in your wider locality with children drawing, for example, different parts of a park. It can also be used as part of work on contrasting localities in the UK or overseas, although children would have to use secondary sources.

(from sheet header) Things I like – things I dislike

Name: _____   Date: _____

This picture is of _____

Things I **like** about this place are _____

Things I **dislike** about this place are _____

This picture is of _____

Things I **like** about this place are _____

Things I **dislike** about this place are _____

Children might compile a list of 'jobs to be done around school' which could form the basis of an action plan for the class to improve the school environment.

Children could also be encouraged to write letters to the headteacher or the chair of governors.

Suggestion(s) for support

If drawing is too difficult, or takes too long, each pair could complete just one worksheet each and later have them photocopied so that they can complete the second half of the activity.

Children could complete the whole activity working with a partner, they could order their drawings together and then compare them with another pair.

Assessment opportunities

Photocopiable page 146 can be used to see whether children understand that an environment can have both attractive and unattractive features and that they can discriminate between them.

Opportunities for IT

The class could make a collection of photographs taken around the school grounds. Each pair of children could take the camera out and photograph the parts of the grounds that they have chosen. These photographs could then be ordered by the children with respect to the quality of the environments they show.

Children could use a scanned version of the photograph within a word processor and write their 'likes' and 'dislikes'

sentences underneath the picture. The final versions could be printed out for display in the classroom, or mounted together into a book for others to read.

Display ideas

Any completed photocopiable sheets, backed with coloured paper, could be displayed on the wall.

It would also be possible to display four poster-style views of very different places. Ask the children to write their names on a piece of paper beneath each one, awarding the view a score between one and ten. This provides an interactive display. Once the whole class has awarded their scores ask some good mathematicians to total each one and write up the winning total to show which view is the favourite.

Other aspects of the Geography PoS covered

Geographical skills – 3a, b, f.
Places – 4c.

Reference to photocopiable sheet

Photocopiable page 146 is central to this activity. It is used to obtain drawings from around the school and has spaces for the children to write their likes and dislikes about each place visited. Children then cut out each of the sections and order them according to their likes and dislikes.

HOW PLACES CHANGE

To appreciate that environments change, sometimes for the better, sometimes for the worse.

†† *Groups of three within a class.*

🕒 *20–30 minutes for the introduction; 30–40 minutes for writing activity; plus extra rôle-play time.*

Previous skills/knowledge needed

Children should be studying a locality – possibly their own school, its locality or a locality elsewhere. As part of the study of that locality they should look at how the quality of the environment is changing. The children should be used to rôle play and should be aware of the places where they are not allowed to go in the school buildings and grounds.

Key background information

When studying localities with children the quality of that locality's environment should be considered. Part of this work should involve looking at how the environment is changing.

It is important that children begin to show an ability to understand not just the way things are but also that they are constantly changing. Work should be of an enquiring nature, so the 'newspaper office' used here provides an ideal vehicle for learning about the real world.

Preparation

Prepare an area of the classroom as a rôle-play newspaper reporters' office. Leave a reasonable amount of display space around the 'office' arranged so that the children can display items themselves. If possible provide some 'props' (see Resources below).

The display space will need to be divided into three parts, one for work on the locality as it is now, one for work on what is changing, and one for work on what people think about these changes.

Resources needed

A rôle-play area with a toy or old telephone and typewriter, pads of paper, writing implements, the class computer, paper, writing, drawing and colouring materials, clipboards, copies of photocopiable pages 147 and 148.

What to do

Discuss with the children what is changing in or around your school. These changes may include:
▲ building work;
▲ a new use for part of the school;
▲ a new pedestrian crossing near the school;
▲ a new wildlife area;
▲ the closing of a local shop;
▲ the building of new houses near to the school.

Ask the class to choose one of the suggested issues to investigate. Explain to the children that they are going to prepare a newspaper about this issue. Show them the rôle-play area and explain any rules they need to observe.

Put the children into groups of three and ask each group to discuss the change which is being considered.

Each group should then produce three pieces of work for display in the 'newspaper office' as follows:
▲ what are things like now;
▲ what is changing;
▲ what people think about the change.

These pieces of work can be in any form, written, pictures, answers to prepared questions or pieces of writing by other people.

The children may wish to interview someone (perhaps a parent or the headteacher). They could use a portable tape recorder to collect the responses to their questions.

As the children complete pieces of work help them to display these in the relevant parts of the display area in the 'newspaper office'.

Photocopiable pages 147 and 148 can be used to help children gather and organise their information.

Suggestion(s) for extension

Photocopiable page 148 can be used to extend the work. Children can use this individually to create their own front page.

Children could use the school camera to take photographs for the display or their individual work. The rôle-play area can be a stimulus for further work about newspapers and for descriptive and report writing.

Suggestion(s) for support

Photocopiable page 147 offers a simple form which children can use to help them collect the information they need on an issue of change in their school or wider environment.

Assessment opportunities

The written work produced by the children can provide evidence of their understanding of how the environment under consideration is changing. The photocopiable pages 147 and 148 can provide evidence for each individual child.

Opportunities for IT

The children could use a word processor, simple desk-top publishing package or dedicated newspaper package to produce their newspaper. The structure of the newspaper could be set up in advance by the teacher and saved to provide a template for use by the whole class. Children could experiment with different-sized fonts and styles for the headlines and sub-headings. Try to provide opportunities for children to originate their writing on the computer; if they have access to simple laptops the writing of stories for the newspaper can be done away from the computer with the desk-top publishing software and the stories 'imported' into

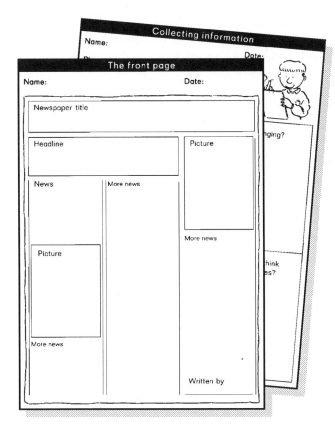

The front page

Name: _____ Date: _____

Newspaper title

Headline | Picture

News | More news

More news

Picture

More news

Written by

Collecting information

Name:

Date:

...ging?

...think
...es?

COULD IT BE BETTER?

To recognise that the quality of an environment can be sustained and improved.

†† *Small groups within a class.*

🕐 *30 minutes for a walk in the school grounds; 40 minutes for group modelling.*

Previous skills/knowledge needed

Children should have spent some time looking at plan views of their school and should be familiar with their school grounds. Some modelling skills are needed.

Key background information

Children must learn that environments change through time, sometimes for the better and sometimes for the worse. They will also begin to realise that opinions differ over such issues.

This activity begins to teach children that people can influence what happens in the world, so we can intervene to sustain situations or even actively improve them.

In the activity the children build a model of the school and its surrounding grounds, including the areas where cars are parked, the school entrances, places where children play and the outside waste bins.

Preparation

Prepare a large-scale map of the school and its grounds. This can be a simple outline shape of the school and the boundaries and pathways around it. Include gateways, the school car-parking area and any other obvious features which you would be able to see from the air.

Encourage the children to collect junk boxes and other modelling materials.

Cut two bases from card to represent the school grounds. If possible make these the same scale as the map. Draw outlines of the features mentioned above using marker pen or something similar.

What to do

Show the children the large-scale map and ask them to identify places on it. Then take the children on a walk around the school grounds, noting on a piece of paper anything that they think should be added to the map. Waste bins, benches,

---

the master document later on for formatting and presentation.

Pictures could be added, either from scanned photographs or pupils' own drawings or from photographs taken by the children themselves and put on to a Kodak CD-ROM.

The children could also use tape recorders to collect information for the newspaper.

Display ideas

The activity generates its own display with the writing and picture work displayed on boards or the wall to the rear and the 'newspaper office' rôle-play area in front. The whole area should provide an on-going interactive learning space centred around the issue of change being studied.

Remember to display any other resources, such as photographs and plans, as a part of the overall display.

Other aspects of the Geography PoS covered

Geographical skills – 2; 3b, f.
Place – 4.

Reference to photocopiable sheets

Photocopiable page 147 can be used by the children to support them as they gather information. They can write a sentence and/or draw a picture in each of the boxes.

Photocopiable page 148 is a blank newspaper front page with spaces for pictures and text which can be used as a stand-alone activity. Children can produce their own front page about the issue under investigation or about other issues.

play equipment, signboards, trees, fences and such things as the school pond, if you have one, should be noted.

Back in the classroom decide where these things are on the map and mark them.

Tell the children that they are going to make two models of the school and its grounds using the base boards that have already been prepared. Try to ensure that the same materials are used for each model so that the two versions are as near identical as possible.

Talk to the children about the school entrances, the waste bins, the seating provision, the play areas, the car parking and the garden or wildlife areas. Get their opinions on these things:
▲ are they a waste of space?
▲ do they serve their purpose adequately?
▲ could they use some improvement?

Arrange the children into two sets of small groups (three or four children per group will work best). One set of groups adds all the items of detail on to one model so that it represents the school as it is now. The other set of groups starts modelling the school grounds as they would like to see them. Half way through this practical part of the activity the groups could swap over so that each half of the class has an opportunity to work on both models. When they have finished, one model will represent the school as it is in reality while the other will show the school with any changes that the children think would improve it.

Photocopiable page 149 could be used to help the children keep a check on the things they have removed, the things they have left the same and any new things they have added.

Suggestion(s) for extension
Children could write explanations of the changes they would like to make and could draw or paint any new features of the new, improved school. If they come up with genuinely sensible and practical ideas, the children could write letters to the headteacher explaining their suggestions.

Suggestion(s) for support
Some children will find the idea of modelling features which do not exist very strange and very difficult. Support them by encouraging them to draw simple design drawings. Let them do this on their own, then pair them with children who are more confident at modelling.

Young children will need items on the large-scale map to be marked with very pictorial symbols.

Assessment opportunities
Photocopiable page 149 will give very good evidence of whether the child understands that decisions were made that involved:
▲ removing certain features which were redundant;
▲ leaving features which were serving their purpose;
▲ adding new features to enhance the school's environment.

Opportunities for IT
Children could use a word processor to write about the changes that they have made to the two models. They could explain what they have done, why, and how it has improved the school. These could be presented as stand-up cards so that they can be displayed alongside the model.

Older or more able children may be able to use a simple graphics package to plan out their improvements. The teacher could draw a plan of the school and save this as a master file which the children could use to show their improvements, possibly making a key and marking each improvement in a different colour.

Display ideas
Display the finished models together with a wall display behind them which explains the 'before and after' idea. Include any art work, design drawings and letters written by children in the display. The large-scale map should also be included.

Other aspects of the Geography PoS covered
Geographical skills – 2.
Places – 4; 5d.
Thematic study – 6a, b.

Reference to photocopiable sheet
Photocopiable page 149 provides three large boxes for the children to draw and write about which things they would remove, which things they would leave as they are and which things they would add to enhance the school grounds.

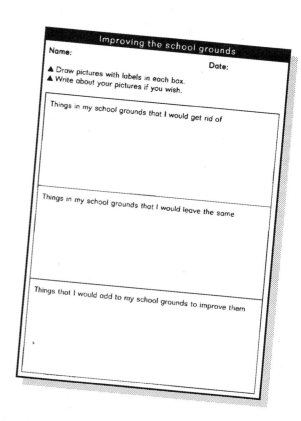

Improving the school grounds

Name:

Date:

▲ Draw pictures with labels in each box.
▲ Write about your pictures if you wish.

Things in my school grounds that I would get rid of

Things in my school grounds that I would leave the same

Things that I would add to my school grounds to improve them

Assessment

Each activity in this book has a section called 'Assessment opportunities'. These sections supply ideas on how the teacher might assess children's learning. Much of this advice centres on formative assessment techniques which often include using the children's photocopiable sheets or other pieces of work as part evidence of ability.

To enhance the opportunities for summative assessment, this section includes eight supplementary summative assessment worksheets. However, it should be remembered that a number of the photocopiable sheets referred to in the first five sections could also be used in a summative way. A list of these is given overleaf.

The following eight activities are based on photocopiable pages 150 to 157. Each activity includes an explanation of its context and how it might best be introduced to the children, a note on how it relates to the PoS and suggestions on the desired outcomes from each activity.

As a good deal of geographical learning at Key Stage 1 is through the child's own environment, much of this type of summative assessment should be viewed in the light of wider geographical work in which the children have been involved.

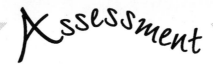

The following photocopiable sheets could also be used for summative assessment.

GEOGRAPHICAL TERMS

Explanation (see page 150)
This is a simple cloze procedure which can be completed independently by able readers or by less able readers who might need the text read to them. The picture supports the children as they place words of geographical relevance.

Reference to PoS
Geographical skills – 3a.

Desired outcome
In cloze procedure the children use clues in the text to help them place the missing words. When analysing the children's responses check whether any inaccurate answers make at least some sense (perhaps 'Driving along the *bridge*' instead of 'Driving along the *road* ').

FOLLOWING DIRECTIONS

Explanation (see page 151)
This activity checks that children are able to follow directions using appropriate terminology. They have to understand *north*, *south*, *east* and *west*, as well as *left* and *right*. They are also required to understand the words *face*, *ahead*, *turn*, *backwards* and *around*.

Explain to the children about counting on and provide support in working with *north*, *south*, *east* and *west* if this is needed. If the children struggle to read the instructions these could be read to them.

Reference to PoS
Geographical skills – 3c.

Desired outcome
The children should end up with a route line which takes the rabbit to the carrot in the bottom left-hand corner.

MAKING MAPS

Explanation (see page 152)
The children are presented with a line drawing which they have to redraw as a map. Some features in the drawing have already been added to the map to help the children get started. Suggest to the children that they imagine that they are up in a helicopter looking down on the school.

Reference to PoS
Geographical skills – 3d.

Desired outcome
Children may want to draw the windows or even the doors which are recessed into the porch and therefore clearly not visible in mapped form. Children who have no problem adjusting their perspective on a view will be able to map the school and the playground as two large inverted 'L' shapes.

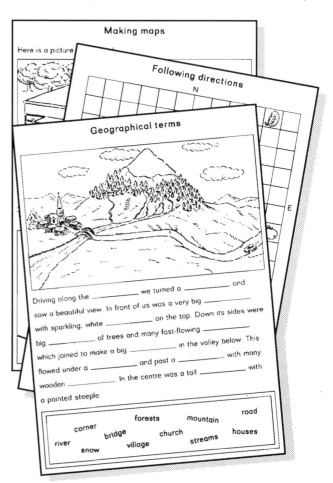

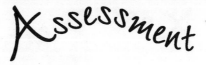

USING MAPS – CIRCUS

Explanation (see page 153)
This activity involves children in using a map to draw a picture of a circus. Emphasise to the children that they must draw the circus as accurately as they can, based on the information they have in the picture, but that their drawing is not a map.

Reference to PoS
Geographical skills – 3e.

Desired outcome
Look for outcomes which show the shapes of the walls of the tent and buildings and for outcomes where the children have managed to place these features in the correct place relative to each other. An excellent outcome would be one where the child has shown features like the shape of the big top's sides and the pathways on the grounds. The best children will be able to depict the details shown on the plan view accurately in their drawings.

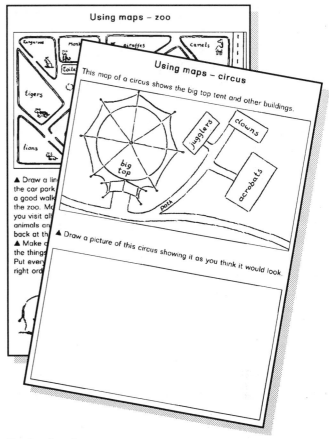

USING MAPS – ZOO

Explanation (see page 154)
The children are asked to draw a route around a map of a zoo, starting and finishing at the car park. This will involve them in interrogating the map and proving their map-use skills. It might help children if they colour all the pathways one colour to start with. Children will want to create quite complex routes so challenge them to make the simplest route they can which passes all of the animals.

Reference to PoS
Geographical skills – 3e.

Desired outcome
A good outcome will be one where a child has drawn a sensible route and has then listed all of the animal pens and other features in the correct order according to the route.

HUMAN AND PHYSICAL FEATURES

Explanation (see page 155)
The children first fill in labels on a picture which shows a range of physical and human geographical features. The words are provided for them. After this, the children decide which are human features and which are physical features by writing them in the appropriate list.

Reference to PoS
Places – 5a.

Desired outcome
Many of the features are clearly identifiable as human or physical features but some could be one or the other, or even both. For example, a child could possibly argue a case for the cliff, the pond or the beach being human features. It is therefore worth talking about each child's completed work.

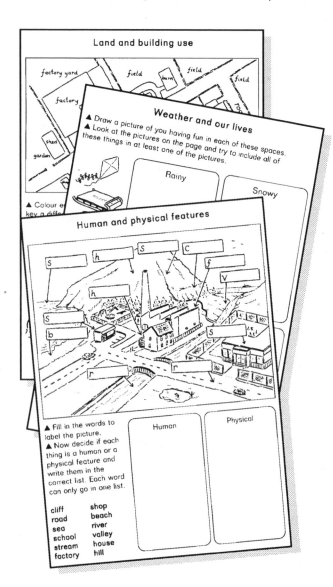

WEATHER AND OUR LIVES

Explanation (see page 156)
This photocopiable sheet shows four types of weather condition and invites the children to draw themselves playing in each type of weather. The children are prompted to include objects from a bank of images displayed down the side of the sheet. Children should write a sentence or a few appropriate words under each of their pictures.

Reference to PoS
Places – 5c.

Desired outcome
A good outcome will have four pictures which clearly show the relevant weather condition and have incorporated appropriate images from the pictures on the sheet.

LAND AND BUILDING USE

Explanation (see page 157)
This activity can be used to determine whether children can distinguish between land and buildings. Using the map they colour-code the different types of land and building use and then tick each usage to indicate whether it is a type of land or a type of building.

Reference to PoS
Places – 5d.

Desired outcome
Ideally a child will have coloured each of the boxes in the key a different colour and then coloured the map accordingly. The 'land' and 'buildings' columns will then be ticked in the correct places.

Photocopiables

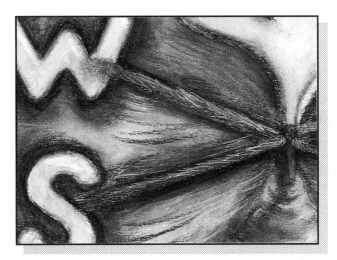

The pages in this section can be photocopied for use in the classroom or school which has purchased this book, and do not need to be declared in any return in respect of any photocopying licence.

They comprise a varied selection of both pupil and teacher resources, including pupil worksheets, resource material and record sheets to be completed by the teacher or children. The photocopiable sheets are related to individual activities in the book; the name of the activity is indicated at the top of the sheet, together with a page reference indicating where the lesson plan for that activity can be found.

Individual pages are discussed in detail within each lesson plan, accompanied by ideas for adaptation where appropriate – of course, each sheet can be adapted to suit your own needs and those of your class. Sheets can also be coloured, laminated, mounted on to card, enlarged and so on where appropriate.

Many sheets have spaces provided for children's names and for noting the date on which each sheet was used. This means that, if so required, they can be included easily within any pupil assessment portfolio.

Photocopiable sheets 150 to 157 accompany the activities in the Assessment chapter; other sheets which can be used for summative assessment have been flagged with the ◈ icon.

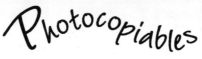
Sketch of our school

Name: **Date:**

This sketch was drawn by	This is who guessed where the place is

This place is _____

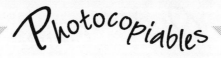

The words we use, see page 15

Word cards

Name: Date:

hill	school	east	right
river	up	north	west
sea	on	down	south
wood	over	off	dark
road	in front of	under	light
house	near	behind	warm
shop	high	far	cold
factory	close	low	quiet
farm	above	distant	noisy
field	apart	below	busy
railway	around	across	wet
canal	left	beside	dry

Big places – little places, see page 17

Different places

Name: Date:

village	town	city

▲ Copy these words in to the correct columns.
Some words might go in more than one column.

market square

railway   flats   town hall

superstore   post office   cinema   park

station   pond

cottage   trees

▲ Add your own words if you can.

Following a route, see page 19

Follow the trail

Name: Date:

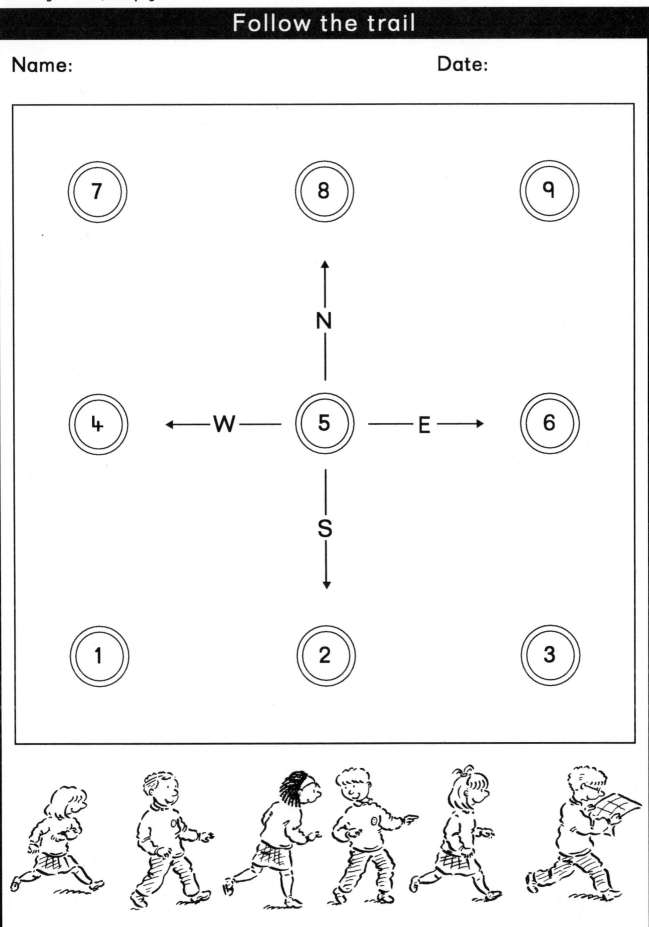

Picture trail, see page 20

Our picture trail

Name: Date:

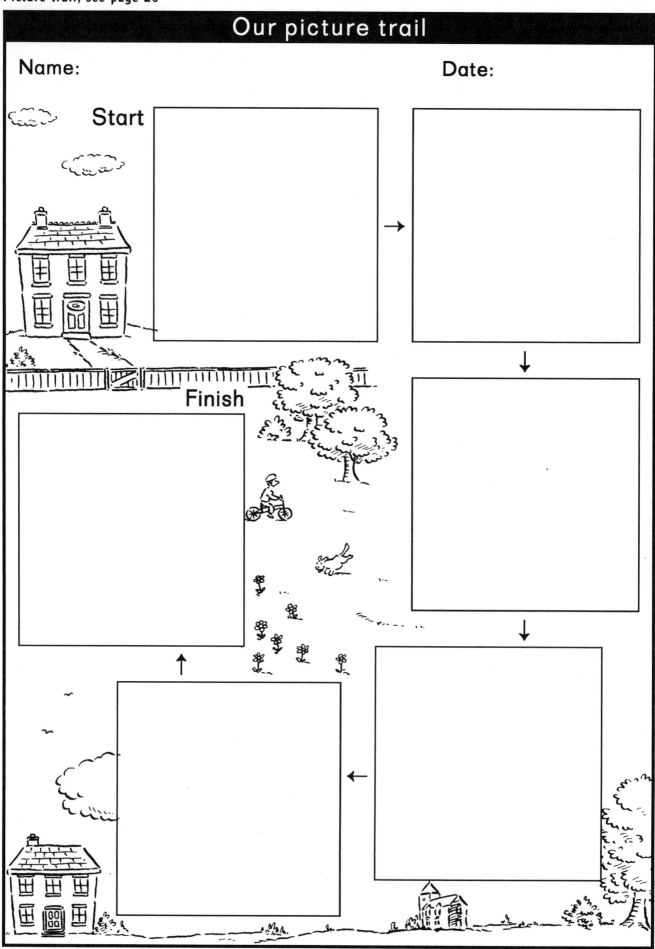

Start

Finish

Take a good look, see page 22

Drawing our school building

Name:

Date:

Things to draw…

windows

doors

roof

gutters

drainpipes

drains

chimneys

signs

A sketch of the .... side of our school building.

Take a good look, see page 22

Data on our school building

Name: **Date:**

My school building

How many?

Classrooms

Teachers

Children

How many?

chimneys

windows

doors

drainpipes

What are they made of?

Walls
stone/cement/brick/
wood/other

Roof
tiles/slate/wood/other

Chimneys
stone/concrete/brick/other

Window frames
wood/metal/plastic

Door frames
wood/metal/plastic

Drainpipes
plastic/metal/wood

Keeping the traffic moving, see page 24

Traffic flow survey

Name: Date:

The place I surveyed

_____

_____

Number of people
who walked by

The busiest place
in our school

The least busy place
in our school

Why is this place busy?

_____

_____

_____

Why is this place not busy?

_____

_____

_____

Secondary sources, see page 26

Recording sheet

Name:

Date:

I am looking for a new/old house made of stone/brick with/without a garden

and with 1/2/3/4/5/6 bedrooms. (Circle each of your choices)

House address	how old?		made of?		garden?		bedrooms						Tick if it suits you.
	new	old	stone	brick	yes	no	1	2	3	4	5	6	

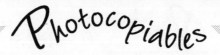
Looking down from the sky

Name: Date:

1	2	3
map view	photograph view	name of feature

▲ Look at the map and the aerial photograph.
▲ Copy the features on the map in the first column.
▲ Copy the features on the photograph in the second column.
▲ Write the name of the feature in the third column.

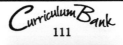

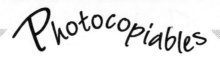

Side view – plan view, see page 33

Side view – plan view cards

Name: Date:

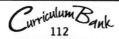

Classroom maps, see page 35

Planning a classroom

Name: Date:

▲ Look at the furniture at the bottom of this sheet.
▲ Colour each square in the key a different colour
and shade the floor areas on the plan.
▲ Cut out the pieces of furniture and stick them on
the plan of the classroom.

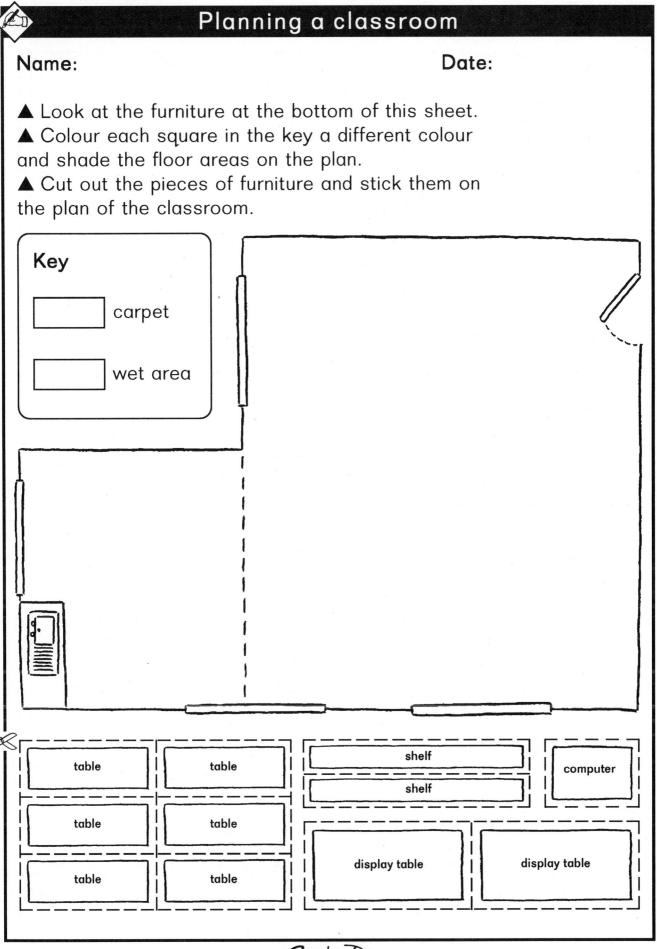

Key

carpet

wet area

table	table
table	table
table	table

shelf
shelf

display table   display table

computer

Let's make a map!, see page 37

Mapping our school building

Name:

Date:

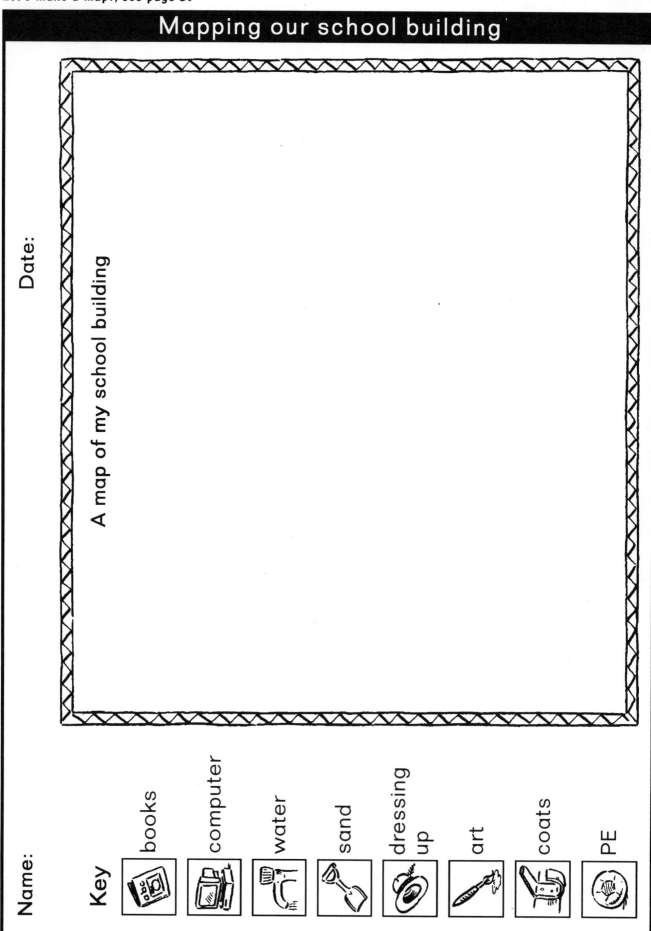

A map of my school building

Key

books

computer

water

sand

dressing up

art

coats

PE

GEOGRAPHY KS1

Let's make a map!, see page 37

Mapping a bedroom

Name: **Date:**

Look at this picture of a bedroom.

▲ Draw a plan of the room in the space below.

▲ Make a key and use symbols to show where the teddy, chair and lamp are on your plan.

Key

teddy

chair

lamp

Pictures and symbols, see page 39

Bedroom plan view

Name: **Date:**

pictures

▲ Draw two *plan views* of your bedroom.
▲ Draw the things in your bedroom as *pictures* in the first drawing.

▲ Draw them as *symbols* and make a *key* in your second drawing.

symbols

Key

GEOGRAPHY KS1

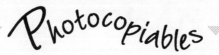

Farm maps

Name: Date:

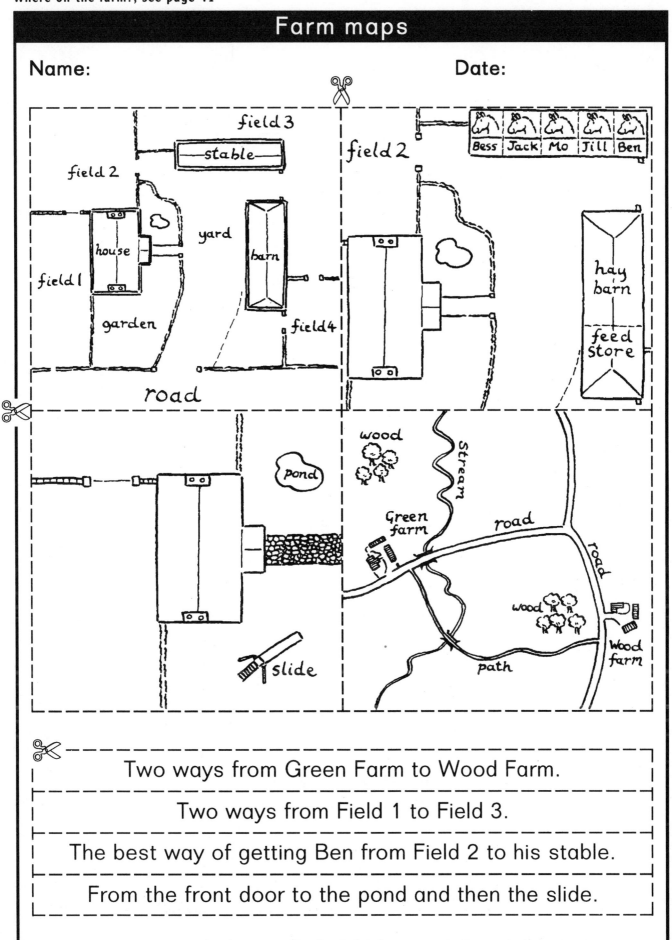

Two ways from Green Farm to Wood Farm.

Two ways from Field 1 to Field 3.

The best way of getting Ben from Field 2 to his stable.

From the front door to the pond and then the slide.

All at different scales, see page 43

Map window

Name: **Date:**

	map 1	map 2	map 3	map 4
the whole world				
whole continents				
seas				
whole countries				
cities as dots				
roads as lines				
villages				
woods				
rivers as lines				
buildings as rectangles				
roads and streets				
buildings in detail				
walls and fences				
trees on their own				
house doorways				
car parking places				

cut this out and look
through the window

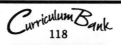
GEOGRAPHY KS1

Globes and world maps, see page 45

Continents of the world

Date:

Name:

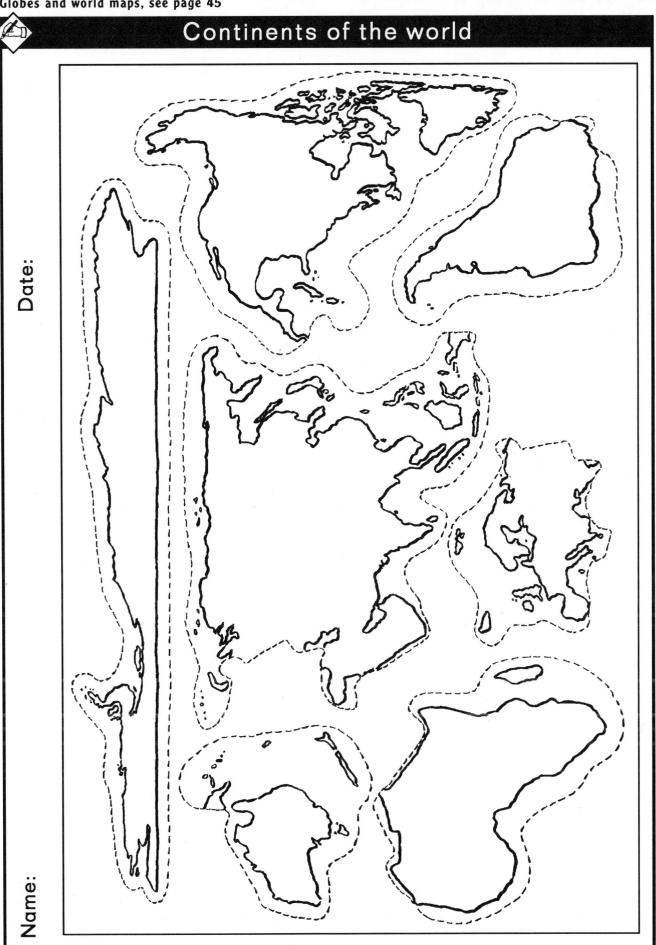

The United Kingdom, see page 47

The British Isles

Name: Date:

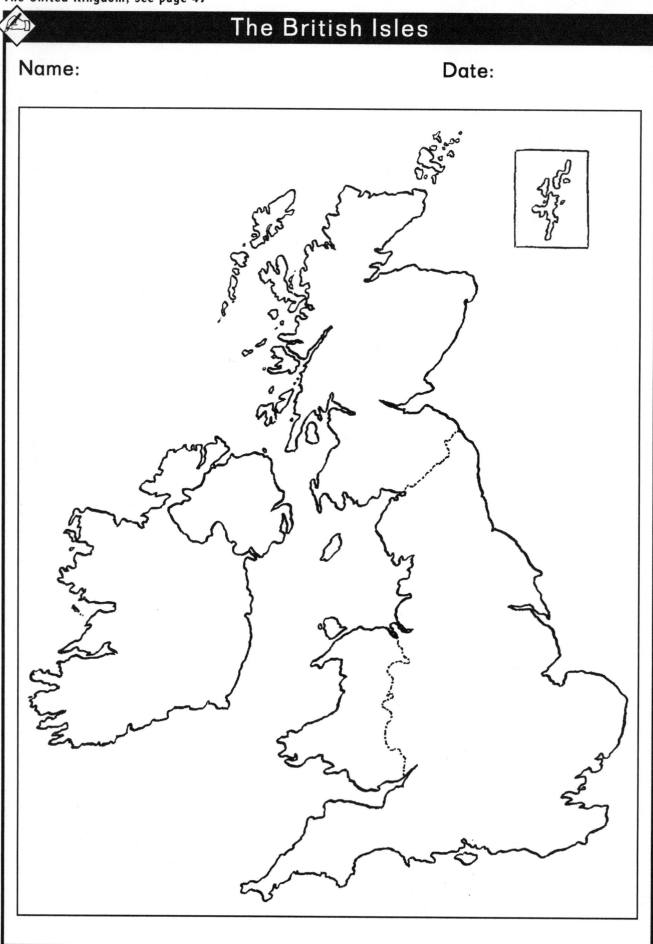

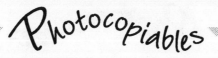

The United Kingdom, see page 47

Countries of the British Isles

Name: Date:

Where do you live?, see page 49

My home

Name: Date:

My home.

My address is

Where I live in my local area.

My local area is called

Where I live in the British Isles.

My nearest town or city is

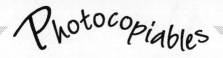
Designing a route

Name: **Date:**

A map of my classroom

Draw coloured lines in the boxes to show which route is which.

Key for routes

⬜	My place to the art corner.
⬜	The art corner to the door.
⬜	Door to the book/reading corner.
⬜	Book/reading corner to the computer.
⬜	Computer to my friend's place.
⬜	My friend's place to my place.
⬜	Longest part of the route.

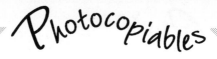
Your locality, see page 56

Features in your locality

Name: **Date:**

	Tick if in your locality
house	
mountain	
church	
factory	
post box	
food shop	
doctor's surgery	
synagogue	
river	
forest	
clothes shop	
mosque	

	Tick if in your locality
telephone box	
hospital	
post office	
temple	
filling station	
café	
field	
bank	
secondary school	
bridge	
cemetery	
park	

GEOGRAPHY KS1

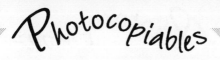

Physical features in your locality

Name: **Date:**

▲ If you have these features in your
locality, draw what each place is like.
▲ Put a cross if you don't have the feature.

highest place	lowest place	valley
stream or river	pond or lake	sea
beach or cliff	wood or forest	stone outcrop

The physical locality, see page 58

Physical and human features in your locality

Name: Date:

▲ Colour around the pictures – green for physical features, red for human features.
▲ Copy the green and red letters into the spaces at the bottom of the sheet to find the two words.

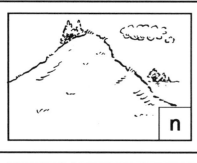
n

p

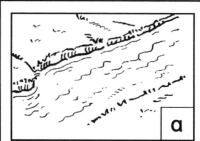
a

e

o

t

u

SPUD SHOP
p

r

l

e

e

Green letters ___ ___ ___ ___ ___

Red letters ___ ___ ___ ___ ___ ___

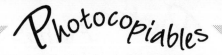
The human locality, see page 60

Human features in your locality

Name: Date:

These places have all been made by people.

▲ Colour the ones you have in your locality.
▲ Write the words in the correct places.

Grocer

house	factory	shop
road	garage	garden
farm	school	playground

GEOGRAPHY KS1

Our sense of place, see page 61

Character of your locality

Name: Date:

On my way to school I see | buildings
fields
mountains
sea | .

Around me I see | houses
flats
shops
factories
farms
churches | .

The land is | hilly
flat | .

It is very | busy
quiet | .

The school locality

Pride in your place, see page 63

A banner for your local area

Name: Date:

GEOGRAPHY KS1

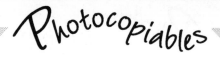

Here is the weather, see page 65

The weather in your locality

Name: Date:

A good day in summer	A poor day in summer
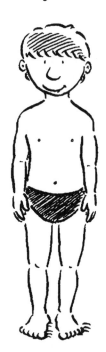	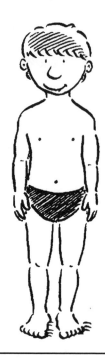

A good day in winter	A poor day in winter
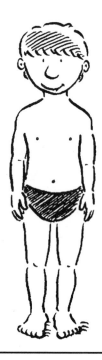	

GEOGRAPHY KS1

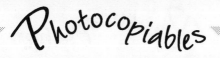

The story of the weather, see page 67

Weather chart

Name: **Date:**

	morning	afternoon
Monday		
Tuesday		
Wednesday		
Thursday		
Friday		

Curriculum Bank

131

GEOGRAPHY KS1

The story of the weather, see page 67

Weather story

Name: Date:

▲ Draw your weather story in these boxes.
When you have finished you could write your
story in words on the back of this sheet.

Monday	Tuesday

Wednesday	Thursday

Friday	

GEOGRAPHY KS1

The weather around you, see page 69

Happytown map

Name:

Date:

Here is a map of Happytown.

▲ Colour the places you would go in summer red.
▲ Colour the places you would go in winter blue.

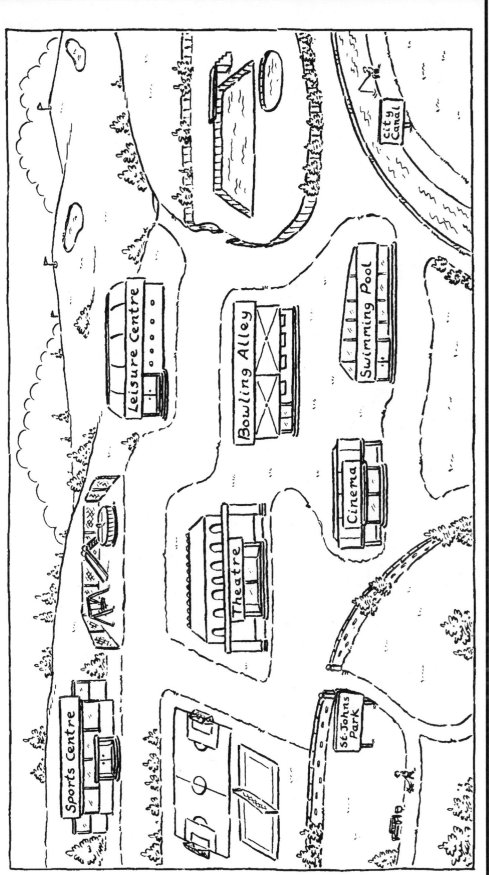

GEOGRAPHY KS1

The weather around you, see page 69

Leisure facilities

Name: Date:

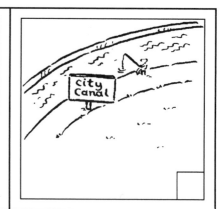

GEOGRAPHY KS1

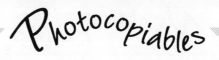

Playground planning, see page 71

Design a playground

Name: Date:

▲ Cut out the activities and fit them in this playground.

Climbing frame

Slide

See-saw

Roundabout

Swings

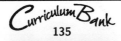

GEOGRAPHY KS1

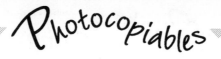

How is it used?, see page 73

Land and buildings in your local area

Name: **Date:**

▲ Draw two buildings from your area.
What is each building? Who lives or works there? What is it for?

This is _____

Who lives or works here? _____

What happens here? _____

This is _____

Who lives or works here? _____

What happens here? _____

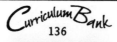

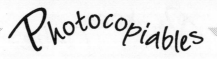

Pictures of places

Name: **Date:**

	same	different

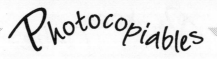

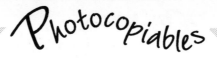

Other localities, see page 78

Living in another locality

Name: | Date:

the land	the people
the weather	the buildings

▲ What is this place called? _____

▲ Where is it? _____

What do you think it would be like to live here?

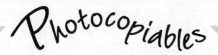
Physical clues, see page 80

Physical features in other localities

Name: Date:

mountains hilly flat	**What I think it looks like**
inland on the coast island	
dry ground streams big river	
rocky ground sandy ground soil	
few plants lots of plants plants and trees	

mountains hilly flat	**Now I know what it looks like**
inland on the coast island	
dry ground streams big river	
rocky ground sandy ground soil	
few plants lots of plants plants and trees	

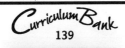

Human features in other localities

Name: **Date:**

My picture of where
I am starting from

My picture of where
I am finishing

My route

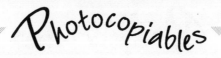

What's it really like?, see page 83

Character of other localities

Name: Date:

Greetings from

your message

affix
stamp
here

address

_____

_____

_____

_____

_____

How's your weather?, see page 85

Weather symbols

Name: Date:

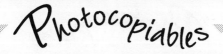

Weather report

Name: **Date:**

My weather forecast

Useful words

sunny

raining

cloudy

windy

snowing

hailing

cold

warm

freezing

hot

foggy

misty

thunder

lightning

Clothes you should wear

Good places to go

People who will need to know

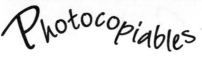

Model places, see page 87

Planning a building

Name: **Date:**

▲ Draw the front and back of the building.
▲ Draw lines linking the labels to your drawing. Fill in the boxes.

The front of my building

The walls are made of

_____

The windows are

_____

The roof is made of

_____

The main door is made of

_____

steps	porch	signs

The back of my building

Is there a chimney?

_____

What colour are the walls?

_____

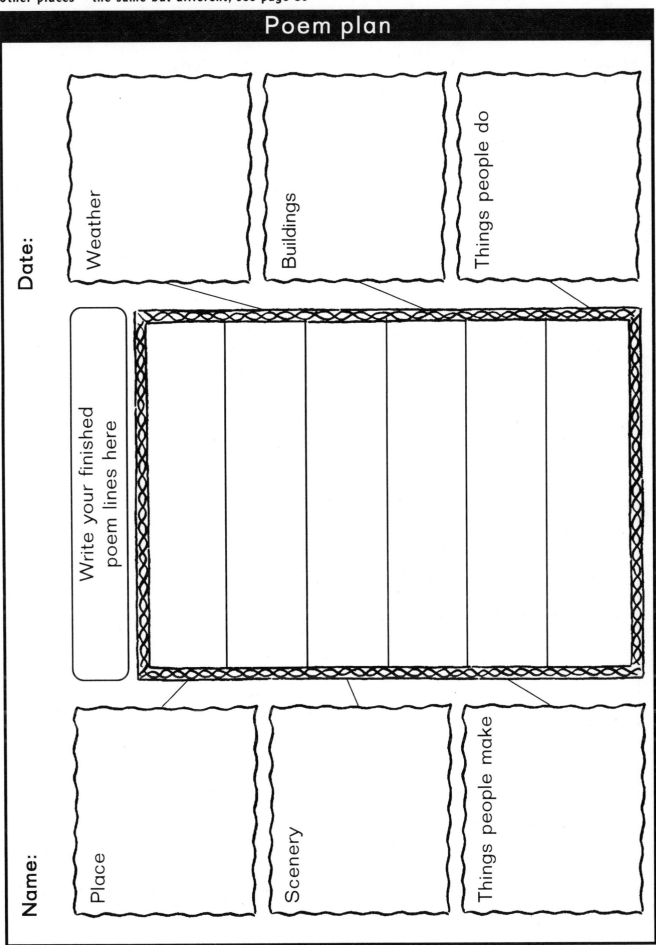

Poem plan

Name:

Date:

Place

Scenery

Things people make

Weather

Buildings

Things people do

Write your finished poem lines here

Likes and dislikes, see page 92

Things I like – things I dislike

Name: Date:

This picture is of _____

Things I **like** about this place are _____

Things I **dislike** about this place are _____

This picture is of _____

Things I **like** about this place are _____

Things I **dislike** about this place are _____

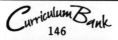

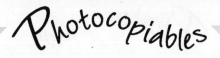
Collecting information

Name: Date:

Place being studied

_____

What is the place like now?	What is changing?
What will it be like?	**What do people think about the changes?**

GEOGRAPHY KS1

How places change, see page 93

The front page

Name: Date:

Newspaper title

Headline

Picture

News   More news

Picture

More news

Picture

More news

Written by

_____

GEOGRAPHY KS1

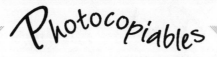

Could it be better?, see page 95

Improving the school grounds

Name: **Date:**

▲ Draw pictures with labels in each box.
▲ Write about your pictures if you wish.

Things in my school grounds that I would get rid of

Things in my school grounds that I would leave the same

Things that I would add to my school grounds to improve them

GEOGRAPHY KS1

Geographical terms, see page 98

Geographical terms

Driving along the _____ we turned a _____ and

saw a beautiful view. In front of us was a very big _____

with sparkling, white _____ on the top. Down its sides were

big _____ of trees and many fast-flowing _____

which joined to make a big _____ in the valley below. This

flowed under a _____ and past a _____ with many

wooden _____ . In the centre was a tall _____ with

a pointed steeple.

corner	forests	mountain	road
river	bridge	church	
snow	village	streams	houses

Following directions, see page 98

Following directions

N

W   E

S

This rabbit is going into its warren for some food.

▲ Follow the directions to find which route it takes.

▲ Draw a line to show the way it goes and a circle around the food it finds.

1 face north	**8** go ahead 3	**15** go ahead 3
2 go ahead 3	**9** go backwards 5	**16** face east
3 turn right	**10** face north	**17** go ahead 2
4 go ahead 2	**11** go ahead 4	**18** turn around
5 turn left	**12** face west	**19** move ahead 3
6 go ahead 2	**13** go ahead 5	**20** turn left
7 turn right	**14** turn south	**21** go ahead 6

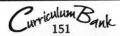
GEOGRAPHY KS1

Making maps, see page 98

Making maps

Here is a picture of a school.

▲ Draw a map of the school in the box below.
The pond and the trees have already been marked.

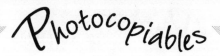

Using maps – circus

This map of a circus shows the big top tent and other buildings.

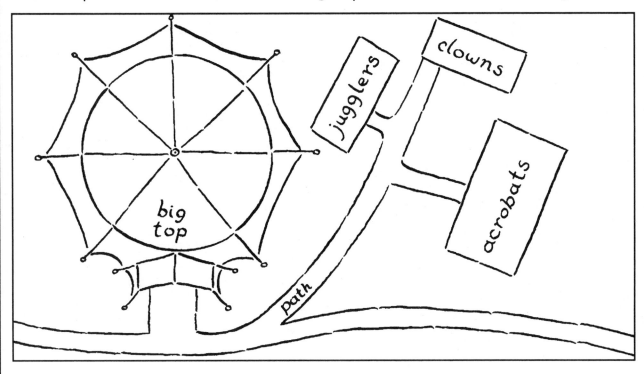

▲ Draw a picture of this circus showing it as you think it would look.

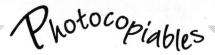

Using maps – zoo, see page 99

Using maps – zoo

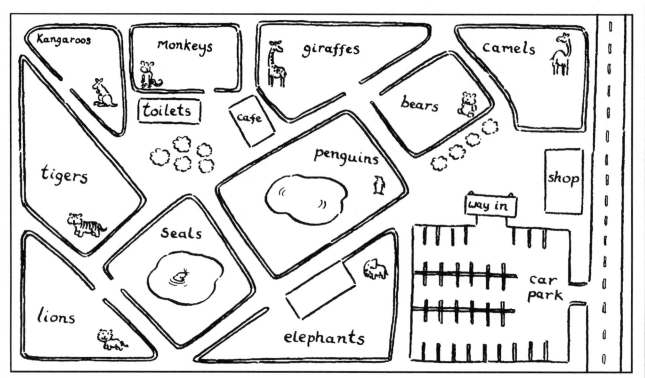

▲ Draw a line from the car park to show a good walk around the zoo. Make sure you visit all the animals and end up back at the car park.
▲ Make a list of all the things you pass. Put everything in the right order.

Things to see at the zoo:

1 car park	8
2	9
3	10
4	11
5	12
6	13
7	14
	15

Human and physical features, see page 99

Human and physical features

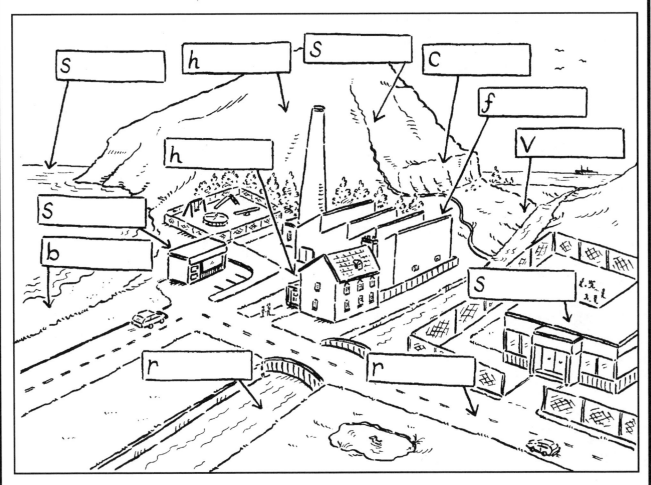

▲ Fill in the words to label the picture.

▲ Now decide if each thing is a human or a physical feature and write them in the correct list. Each word can only go in one list.

Human	Physical

cliff   shop
road   beach
sea   river
school   valley
stream   house
factory   hill

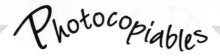

Weather and our lives

▲ Draw a picture of you having fun in each of these spaces.
▲ Look at the pictures on the page and try to include all of
these things in at least one of the pictures.

Rainy	Snowy
Sunny	Windy

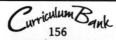

Land and building use

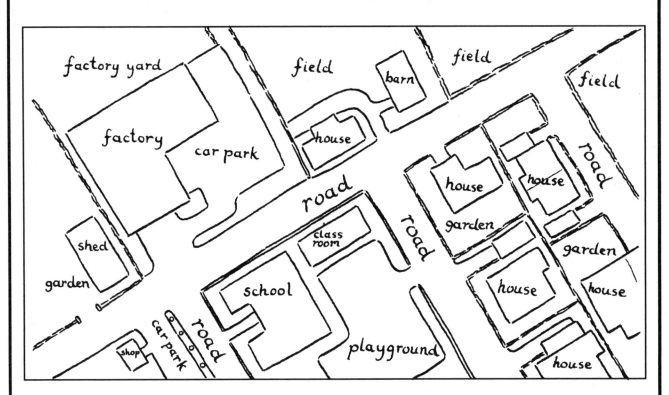

▲ Colour each part of the key a different colour. Then colour the map, using the right colours.
▲ Tick whether each item in the key is land or building.

Key		Land	Building
	houses		
	gardens		
	fields		
	barns		
	schools		
	playgrounds		
	shops		
	car parks		
	sheds		
	factories		
	factory yards		
	roads		

GEOGRAPHY KS1

INFORMATION TECHNOLOGY WITHIN GEOGRAPHY AT KEY STAGE 1

The information technology activities outlined in this book can be used to develop and assess children's IT capability as outlined in the National Curriculum. Types of software rather than names of specific programs have been mentioned to enable teachers to use the ideas regardless of which computer they are using.

Main IT focus

The main emphasis for the development of IT capability within these activities is on communicating and handling information. Within this strand the use of drawing or art software is particularly important.

Art packages

A number of simple art or graphics packages, suitable for children, are available across a wide range of computers. These tend to fall into two categories.

The first are graphics packages which enable children to draw lines and shapes and add text. The lines and shapes can be manipulated, by re-sizing, moving, stretching and rotating them. Colours can be changed and shapes filled.

On more sophisticated packages shapes can be combined to form one object so that, for example, all the components of a house can be drawn separately, then combined and kept as a house. Text can be typed on the page and some packages have different fonts, sizes and colours. It is easy to move shapes around the screen and position components of a picture wherever you wish. These packages are sometimes referred to as vector graphics drawing software.

Art or painting packages use a different approach, but often achieve the same or similar results. The drawing process is more like using a pencil or brush. Lines and shapes are drawn by colouring in the individual pixels on the screen. Very detailed work and special effects can be produced to create pictures which mirror the results of paint on paper.

These packages usually have a range of tools such as brushes, sprays and rollers for adding and creating different effects. Text can be added, coloured and resized. The scanned images that children make using a hand scanner can be combined in such packages and edited, changing colours or masking out parts of the picture. This type of package is often referred to as a pixel painting package.

The skills that children need to be taught to use this type of software are similar to those needed for word-processing, but related to pictures. They will need to know how to:
▲ select appropriate drawing tools;
▲ change features such as line thickness;
▲ draw different lines and shapes;
▲ edit and erase shapes and lines;
▲ resize and rotate shapes and lines;
▲ move shapes and lines around the screen;
▲ select and add colours;
▲ add, resize and colour text;
▲ save and retrieve their work from a disk;
▲ set up the printer and print out their work.

Kodak CD-ROMs

Pictures taken using a conventional camera can now be transferred onto a special CD-ROM using a system developed by Kodak; hence the name.

Once photographs have been developed and printed you can select up to 100 different pictures, take these to a branch of Boots the Chemists, and ask for them to be put onto a Kodak CD-ROM. The initial cost for the CD-ROM with 24 pictures is around £25, but each extra photo added after that costs about 60p. It is not essential to produce all 100 photos at the same time as new pictures can be added to the disk at a later stage. Check that your CD player is multi-session as this will enable it to find the photos which are added later. Most CD players are now of this kind.

The images that are displayed on the screen are very high quality and they can be used within different applications that accept this image form, such as word processors, desktop publishing and art or drawing packages. The children can use these as part of writing or presentation or for art work. The pictures can be printed out using a colour printer or parts of the picture can be 'captured' and used within a worksheet or as a stimulus for other geography work.

This new storage form provides schools with a unique way of building up collections of pictures linked to specific topics in geography. They might include:
▲ pictures of the school and locality;
▲ pictures related to contrasting localities;
▲ pictures to illustrate different physical or human features.

Mixing different forms of information

There are now many computer packages which allow children to mix together different kinds of information, often text and pictures. Key Stage 1 children can be shown how to place a picture into their work and add appropriate text. Pictures can be obtained from several sources:
▲ collections of clip art from disks or CD-ROMs (such as *Treasure Chest*);
▲ pictures children draw with art or drawing packages;
▲ children's pictures which have been scanned into an electronic format using a hand scanner;
▲ collections of photographs put onto Kodak CD-ROM.

The grids on page 159 relate the activities in this book to specific areas of IT and to relevant software resources. Activities are referenced by page number, and bold page numbers indicate activities which have expanded IT content. The software listed is a selection of programs generally available to primary schools, and is not intended as a recommended list.

AREA OF IT	SOFTWARE	ACTIVITIES (PAGE NOS.)				
		CHAPTER 1	CHAPTER 2	CHAPTER 3	CHAPTER 4	CHAPTER 5
Communicating Info	Word processor	14, 15, 20, 26	33, 49, 51	56, 60, **61**, 69, 71, 75	78, 82, 83, 85, 89	92, 93, 95
Communicating Info	DTP	17			83	**93**
Communicating Info	Concept keyboard		33	61		
Communicating Info	Drawing package	15, 22	**35**, 37, 39, 41, 45, 47, 49	63		95
Communicating Info	Painting package	15, 26	**45**, 49	61, 65, 71		
Communicating Info	Framework	17	32, 37		**87**	
Communicating Info	Kodak CD-ROM	20		56, 58, 60, 63, 69, 75	80	93
Communicating Info	Multi-media		33	58, 63		
Information Handling	Database	22, 24, **26**		**67**, 73	78	
Information Handling	Graphing software	22		56, 60, 67		
Information Handling	CD-ROM	15, 29	32		78, 87, 89	
Control	ROAMER/PIPP	**19**	51, **53**			
Control	Tape recorder			69	89	
Control	Video-still camera	14, 20, 22	33, 41	**56**, 58, 71, 73	80	92

SOFTWARE TYPE	BBC/MASTER	RISCOS	NIMBUS/186	WINDOWS	MACINTOSH
Word processor	*Stylus* *Folio* *Prompt/Writer*	*Phases* *Pendown* *Desk Top Folio*	*All Write* *Write On*	*My Word* *Kid Works 2* *Creative Writer*	*Kid Works 2* *EasyWorks* *Creative Writer*
DTP	*Front Page Extra*	*Desk Top Folio* *1st Page*	*Front Page Extra* *NewSPAper*	*Creative Writer* *NewSPAper*	*Creative Writer*
Framework		*My World*		*My World*	
Art package		*1st Paint* *Kid Pix* *Splash*		*Colour Magic* *Kid Pix 2*	*Kid Pix 2*
Drawing package	*Picture Builder*	*Draw* *Picture IT*	*Picture Builder*		
Authoring		*Hyperstudio* *Rainbow*		*Hyperstudio* *MM Box*	*Hyperstudio*
Database	*Our Facts* *Grass* *Pigeonhole* *Datashow*	*DataSweet* *Find IT*	*Our Facts* *Datashow*	*Sparks* *ClarisWorks* *Information Workshop*	*ClarisWorks* *EasyWorks*
Graphing software	*Datashow*	*Pictogram* *Picture Point* *Data Sweet*	*Datagraph*	*Datagraph* *EasyWorks*	*EasyWorks*

GEOGRAPHY KS1

	ENGLISH	MATHEMATICS	SCIENCE	HISTORY	D & T	IT	ART	MUSIC	PE	RE
EARLY GEOGRAPHICAL SKILLS	Geographical vocabulary in speaking, listening, reading and writing. Giving and following directions.	Measuring space and area in non-standard and standard units. Right angles. Simple scales on, for example, a thermometer.	Fieldwork exploring materials in the locality. Using scientific processes in studying, for example, the weather.	Geographical and historical words. Fieldwork activity looking at change through time. Use of secondary sources.	Use of geographical terms in designing geography-based posters. Making simple weather recording instruments.	Using IT to communicate and handle information. Using graphics, writing and information packages.	Using observational skills to help appreciate places. Recording places using painting, collage, sculpture, etc.	Recording and responding to sounds present in the environment as a fieldwork activity.	Spatial awareness and developing spatial skills through games, gymnastic activity and dance.	Geographical terminology and the teaching of religious stories. Pictures and other secondary sources on places to enhance RE.
MAPPING	Mapping as a context for reading and writing words connected with location, direction and place names.	Measuring, space and scale in map work. Scaling up and down. Identifying shapes. Turning 3D shapes into 2D.	Trails/mapping activities on the theme of materials in the environment. Mapping living things and their habitats.	Using historical maps of the locality and other localities.	Designing and evaluating maps and models of places. Making three-dimensional models of, for example, the school.	Drawing maps on the computer. Accessing simple maps using software packages incl. CD-ROM and the Internet.	Making maps using skills developed within the art curriculum (handling media and materials).	Mapping sounds in the school grounds and locality.	Using simple apparatus plans. Using plans to explain large area games.	Using maps to learn about holy places and locations referred to in religious stories.
STUDYING YOUR LOCALITY	Description of features. Spoken or written work on local features or people. Reading resources about the local area.	Space, area and shapes in the environment. Measuring in map work in the locality. Collecting and handling primary data.	Materials in your locality. Use of electricity in your locality. Forces and motion. Light/dark and noisy/quiet places in the local area.	Analysing evidence of change in the locality. Talking to local people about changes.	Designing and making models of shops or houses in the locality. Looking at structures (such as bridges, buildings, play grounds).	Presenting data and information about the local area. Using the computer to handle primary data collected in the local area.	Drawing, painting, collage, sculpting, model-making as methods for recording in the locality. Aesthetics of the locality.	Following a sound trail in the locality. Representing qualities of the locality through musical presentation.	Places used for physical activity in the school grounds and locality.	Places of worship in the school's locality. Understanding the breadth of religious groups or communities in the local area.
STUDYING OTHER LOCALITIES	Interpreting secondary source material. Listening to videos, radio or people from other places. Writing letters to twinned schools.	Comparing sizes, dimensions and shapes of different places. Collecting and handling secondary data on localities.	Contrasting building materials used in different localities. Living things in contrasting localities.	Maps from different periods showing localities studied. Empathising with people from the past in other places.	Design of features in the contrasting localities being studied. Modelling features of contrasting localities.	Obtaining information about distant places using mapping packages, CD-ROM and the Internet.	The artistic traditions of contrasting localities. Features, people and cultures of localities as stimulus for art work.	The musical traditions of contrasting localities being studied. Contrasting localities as a stimulus for making music.	Comparing PE curricula of own school and schools in other places. Physical activity and leisure facilities in other localities.	Traditions and practices of religious communities in contrasting localities being studied. Places of worship in other places.
STUDYING ENVIRONMENTAL QUALITY	Rôle-play, speaking and listening about attractive or unattractive features of the environment. Writing views on local issues.	Using mathematical (eg measuring) skills to support proposals for projects which would improve the environments studied.	Living things in the environment. Protecting or creating habitats as part of work on attractive and unattractive places in the school grounds.	Comparing old and new environments, buildings etc. How the school environment has changed through the school's history.	Designing displays or posters which put over a viewpoint. Designing and making models of features for a school grounds improvement.	Making presentations using the computer to generate pictures and writing. Photographing the school's environment.	Appreciation of the attractive and unattractive qualities of environments. Understanding that different people see the same thing differently.	Performance locations in the school grounds. Noisy and quiet places in the school grounds.	Dance as a medium for feelings about places liked or disliked. Children's ideas about improving the physical environment.	Understanding that different people hold different views on the environment. Places suitable for worship within the school.